cooking the sportsman's harvest

SOUTH DAKOTA DEPARTMENT OF GAME, FISH & PARKS

1974

Christmas 1978 from Bob & Jan

The Game, Fish and Parks Department deeply appreciates the hundreds of recipes contributed for the preparation of this cookbook. These recipes will allow you to prepare some of the finest game and fish meals ever enjoyed by discriminating diners.

We are confident you will find them tantalizing to eat and a challenge to your culinary skills. Some of these recipes have been handed down for generations and come to you from the stove of pioneer settlers who depended upon wild game to sustain them in the settlement of this land.

We regret we were unable to use all the recipes donated to us, but just as there is a limited amount of space in an oven there are a limited amount of pages in a cookbook.

We also thank the South Dakota State University Home Economics Department for its assistance in reviewing and editing the recipes.

FOREWORD

The opening of any fishing or game season has a very special meaning to the angler or hunter. The companionship and thrill of the outing is but part of the total experience—the fruits of the outing must also be enjoyed.

Most sportsmen pride themselves in taking care of their game and making it presentable and tasteful when it comes time to consume these delicacies.

The British like the gamy taste of their fowl. For them proper care after shooting a game bird is to bleed it, keeping the blood for sauces, and then to hang it for a period of time depending on the age of the bird. These birds are hung until the tail feathers can be pulled out easily or until a slight bluish tinge appears on the thin skin of the abdomen. The smaller birds should be picked within 24 hours, and then roasted with the entrails still inside.

The British are very particular about their game and place it in high regard. They enjoy the wild taste of game and take great care in preserving this flavor.

Americans usually differ in this manner. In fact they are almost the complete opposite. They dislike the gamy taste and go through diligent preparations to remove wild flavor.

Their goal is to make the wild game taste like domestic animals and only then will they eat it. However, the first mistake is usually made as soon as the hunter or fishermen takes the animal in the field.

If wild game is not correctly taken care of in the field, no matter how carefully the cook prepares it, it will not be palatable.

Each animal should be cleaned and cooled as soon as possible. Prairie grouse should be drawn before placed in the game bag. Antelope should be drawn, skinned and cooled in a matter of minutes. Fish should be kept alive until ready to clean or cleaned immediately after catching and placed on ice.

Big game animals, especially the larger ones such as elk, are especially receptive to spoiling and if not dressed and cooled immediately will not be fit to eat.

Age of game determines how they shall be cooked. If you are in doubt about the age use a moist heat method of preparation.

Most wild game is leaner than domestic animals and should usually have some added fat when cooking. This can be accomplished by placing the bacon bits inside the meat or bacon strips on tops.

Most light-fleshed fowl is cooked well done and most dark fowl is roasted fast under high heat so the outside is brown, but the inside is rare and juicy.

Care must be taken in removing all fat from deer and antelope. Moose meat is relatively fat and can be cooked like pork. Elk is more like beef then any other game and can be prepared accordingly.

Remember, whatever your specialty—rabbit, pheasant, deer or walleyes—the good sportsman takes good care of his game and fish and prides himself in making it fit for the table.

CONTENTS

Fish

BAKED FISH

2 lbs. fish fillets, thawed and dried
½ cup melted butter (can use margarine)
8 oz. potato chips (crushed fine)
salt and paprika

Dip the seasoned fish in melted butter. Melt the butter in the pan you intend to use. Roll in the finely crushed chips. Lay them in baking pan without overlapping. Sprinkle with paprika and bake at 400° for 40-45 min. or until nicely browned. Serve with lemon wedge or fish sauce. This recipe can be used on any kind of fish. Very good.

Mrs. L. J. Mernaugh, 627 North Jackson, Pierre, S. D. 57501

Note: This recipe can also be used for chicken. Allow about 1 hour cooking time.

Mrs. Leonard Reinke, Box 267, Elkton, S. D. 57026

Variation:
Crushed cereal can be used in place of potato chips.

Rose Paulsen, RR #1, Miller, S. D. 57362

BAKED NORTHERN FILLETS

fish fillets
flour
1 egg
cornflake crumbs
salt and pepper
lemon juice

Line a cookie sheet with foil and rub it generously with butter. Dip each serving of fillet successively in flour, beaten egg and cornflake crumbs and place on foil. Then sprinkle generously with salt and pepper. Place in a 425° oven for 15 minutes. Remove from oven and dribble melted butter on each fillet and sprinkle with lemon juice. Return to a 375° oven and bake for 15-20 minutes more. It is not necessary to turn the fillets when you bake them this way. Lower the temperature until you are ready to serve the fish. Leftover fillets may be frozen and later reheated in oven or broiler.

Note: After Hank Bradshaw sampled this recipe in our home, it was featured in the story "Lake of the Big Pike" in the Jan. 1969 issue of Outdoor Life.

Mrs. Wm. P. Hart, Ft. Pierre, S. D. 57532

BAKED FISH

Freeze fish, preferably trout, separately. Hold fish under hot-water faucet just long enough to loosen skin, then remove skin.

Crush cornflakes or toasties with rolling pin. Dip fish in milk or cream; roll in the crushed flakes. Season and bake in a 500° oven 12-15 minutes, depending on the thickness of the fish. Turn only once.

This will produce a delicious, non-greasy fish. Works well with any kind of fish, even fillets. Fish may also be prepared in this manner without skinning.

Florence Blackburn, Bison, S. D. 57620

Variation:
Melted margarine can be dripped over each piece before baking. Season with lemon juice and paprika in addition to salt and pepper.

Mrs. Leo Guenthner, 1020 S. Main, Redfield, S. D. 57469

BAKED FISH FILLETS

1 qt. fish fillets (such as walleye or perch)
seasoned flour
butter or margarine
evaporated milk

Butter an 8" x 10" pan generously. Roll fish fillets in flour and lay side by side in pan. Dot with butter or margarine and pour evaporated milk over to just about cover. Bake at 375° for 45 min.

Mrs. John Voeltz, Box 100, RR #2, Howard, S. D. 57349

FISH FILLETS WITH HERBS

1½ lb. fish fillets
1 tsp. paprika
1 tsp. parsley
1 tsp. salt
¼ tsp. pepper
1 tbsp. butter
sprinkle of lemon juice
fresh lemon slices

Line baking dish or pan with foil. Place fish gently in pan and sprinkle with seasonings, butter and lemon juice. Bake uncovered at 425° for 18 min. Gently lift foil and transfer fillets into serving dish. Garnish with lemon slices. Serves 6.

Mrs. J. J. Rath, Box "F", Leola, S. D. 57456

BAKED NORTHERN PIKE

2 northern pike, cut in crosswise slices about 2 in. thick
salt and pepper
1 large sweet onion, cut in thick slices
1 (1 lb.) can ready-seasoned stewed tomatoes
1 tsp. dried basil leaves

Place slices of pike in greased baking pan. Season with salt and pepper. Place slices of onion on fish. Spoon tomatoes over onions. Crumble basil over tomatoes. Bake in moderate oven (350°) for about 1 hour or until fish flakes easily. Good served with baked potatoes, carrot casserole and celery, apricot pie for dessert.

Mrs. Kermit Karst, 514 Belmont Drive, Rapid City, S. D. 57701

NORTHERN PIKE

fish
1 onion, chopped
½ green pepper, chopped
2 c. celery diced
2 cans tomatoes

Place scaled but unskinned fish in shallow baking pan. Salt the cavity. In separate skillet saute onion, green pepper and celery. Add tomatoes, mashed slightly, and simmer till well blended. Pour mixture over fish, scooping spoonfuls into cavity. Bake in moderate oven, basting occasionally. Fish is thoroughly baked when gently poked with fork tine, it does not weep.

Serve with baked potatoes, slice of lemon and salad.

Mrs. Robert J. Burckhard, RR #1, Aberdeen, S. D. 57401

BAKED FISH IN TOMATO DILL SAUCE

1 lb. fish fillets (such as perch)
1 cup chopped onion
2 tbsp. butter
1 tbsp. flour
1 can condensed consomme, undiluted
½ cup tomato catsup
¾ cup sliced dill pickle

Heat oven to 400°. Saute onions in butter. Stir in flour; gradually add consomme and catsup. Simmer 25 min., stirring occasionally. Add pickles. Place fish in baking dish (10" x 6" x 1½"), cover with sauce.
Bake 25-30 minutes or until fish flakes easily with a fork. Yield: 4 servings.

Mrs. Therman W. Patzlaff, West View Farm, Alexandria, S. D. 57311

BAKED FISH

1 medium to large fish (bass or northern)
1 can cream of mushroom soup
½ soup can milk
1 tsp. salt

Salt the fish and place in baking dish. Mix soup and milk and pour over the fish. Cover and bake in 350° oven for about 1 hour or until fish is flaky. (Length of time depends upon size of fish.) Cream of celery or cream of chicken soup may be used instead of the mushroom.

Mrs. Keith Louder, Draper, S. D. 57531

BAKED PADDLEFISH SQUARES

Cut as much paddlefish in good serving squares as you like. Butter a baking pan quite well. Dip fish in Shake and Bake; coat well. Lay in rows across the pan, then cover the top of each fish square with more butter. Put in a 375° oven and bake until nice and brown.

Mrs. Clara M. Poynter, Box 52, Oelrichs, S. D. 57763

BOILED FISH

Heat to rolling boil in 8 qt. kettle the following:

4 qts. water
2 tbsp. salt
4 to 6 bay leaves
3 to 4 shakes Tabasco sauce

Add:

2 to 3 lbs. fish, cut in 2" x 4" fillets. Cook until tender or starting to flake. **Do not overcook.** Serve on a hot tray with lemon slices and parsley. Spread some hot lemon butter over fish on the tray and sprinkle with paprika.

Lemon Butter:

Melt ¼ lb. butter with juice of ½ lemon. (Use the other ½ lemon for the slices on the tray with fish.)

Mr. Donald L. Nultemeier, 220 South Dakota, Salem, S. D. 57058

BOILED NORTHERN PIKE

1 lb. fish fillets
2 qts. water
2 tsp. salt
1 tbsp. Liptons onion soup mix
¼ tsp. celery salt

Bring water and seasoning to a boil. Add fish fillets; boil 20 to 25 minutes depending on thickness. Remove; add butter and serve.

Mrs. J. J. Rath, Box "F", Leola, S. D. 57456

FISH CHOWDER

1 c. salt pork or bacon - diced
¾ c. sliced onions
2 c. diced potatoes
2 c. hot water
1½ lbs. fish fillets such as walleye, perch or pickerel
salt and pepper
2 c. half and half cream
butter

Fry the salt pork in a skillet until it is nicely browned. Add the onions and saute them gently. Add the potatoes and hot water and cook them for a few minutes or until the potatoes are partly done. Then add the fish fillets and cook until they are easily flaked with a fork. Season to taste with salt and pepper; add cream. Let it all heat thoroughly and serve in bowls, topping with a pat of butter.

Mrs. J. J. Rath, Box "F", Leola, S. D. 57456

CATFISH SOUP

2 to 3 lbs. catfish, cut up
2 qt. cold water
1 sliced onion
1 chopped stalk celery
salt and pepper
1 bay leaf
little parsley
pinch of thyme
1 c. milk
2 tbsp. butter

Put all ingredients except the milk and butter in a kettle or stewpan and cook over low heat until the meat falls apart. Add milk and butter and bring to a boil. Serve hot .

Mrs. Clara M. Poynter, Box 52, Oelrichs, S. D. 57763
Mrs. Dave Robin, PO Box #463, Upton, Wyoming 82730

CARP CHOWDER

6 lb. carp
1 onion
1 tsp. tarragon
½ lemon, sliced

Poach carp in water with onion, tarragon, sliced lemon with peel left on until fish is nearly done. Remove from heat and pick flesh from the bones.

Chowder:

3 c. carp meat
5 slices of chopped bacon
1 chopped onion
2 c. diced cooked potatoes
1 qt. milk
4 soda crackers, rolled fine
butter
salt and pepper
crushed basil

Brown bacon; remove from skillet; add and saute onions. Remove from fat to drain. Place in pan when drained; add fish; cooked potatoes and heat. To this add the milk. When hot remove from stove and add cracker crumbs, stirring well. Add desired butter and salt and pepper. Top each chowder bowl with crushed basil.
Serve with garlic bread.

Mr. Karl M. Rottluff, M.D., PO Box #1822, Sante Fe, New Mexico 87501

PICKLED FISH

Make a brine of water and salt - 2 c. salt to 1 gal. water.
Have fish skinned and cut in quite small pieces. Soak fish pieces in this brine for 24 hours. Rinse off quickly in cold, fresh water. Pour off immediately.

Mix:

4 c. white vinegar
1 c. water
½ to ⅔ c. sugar
1 tbsp. mixed pickling spices

Heat this slightly and pour over fish. Add sliced lemon and onion.

This can be eaten the following day. Any kind of fish can be used but we prefer to use smaller ones. We have even used paddlefish.

Mrs. Leonard Reinke, Box 267, Elkton, S. D. 57026

CANNED FISH

Clean fish and skin them. Cut into pieces about 2 inches long. Pack in clean pint jars. Add 1 tsp. salt, 3 tbsp. vinegar and 1 drop liquid smoke to each pint. Process in a pressure cooker for 80 minutes at 10 lb. pressure.

Mrs. Earl Ellwanger, Custer State Park, Hermosa, S. D. 57744

CANNED FISH

Any kind of fish can be used such as trout, pike or suckers. Pack chunks of raw fish into pint jars.

Mix together:

1 tsp. salt
¼ c. vinegar
¼ c. Snap-E-Tom tomato cocktail
1 tsp. brown sugar

Pour over fish in jars; seal. Process in pressure cooker at 10 lb. for 90 minutes.

This resembles canned salmon and is very good for fish loaf.

Mrs. Roy W. Cook, Spearfish, S. D. 57783

FISH LOAF

1 pt. canned fish
20 crushed soda crackers
1 beaten egg
1 c. milk

Mix ingredients together and bake in a greased single-loaf bread pan at 350° for 1 hour.

Mrs. Roy W. Cook, Spearfish, S. D. 57783

FINNAN HADDIE

2 lbs. finnan haddie
thin white sauce

Soak finnan haddie for at least 1 hour in water to cover. Drain off water. Wrap fish in cheese cloth and place on rack with 1 cup water in pressure cooker. Place cover on cooker. Allow steam to flow from vent pipe to release all air from cooker. Put indicator weight on vent pipe and cook 7 minutes with stem at COOK position. Let stem return to DOWN position. Serve with a thin white sauce.

Mrs. Ed Markus, Corsica, S. D. 57328

SMOKED FISH

Wash fish in salt water and dry. Brush with melted butter. Sprinkle with celery salt inside and out. Put in very warm smoker until you can pull the dorsel fin out. Cover the coals with hard-wood sawdust. Smoke 1-1½ hours. Eat while still warm.

Clinton S. Nagel, Klammweg #18, 7503 Neureut, Karlsruhe, Germany

BAKED TROUT FILLETS

12 trout fillets
1 egg
⅓ c. evaporated milk
salt and pepper
1 c. crushed cracker crumbs (more if desired)
¼ lb. butter
12 small slices cheddar cheese
3 fresh tomatoes, sliced
juice from 1 lemon

Beat egg, add milk and seasoning. Dip fillets in this and then in cracker crumbs. Put butter in skillet and brown fillets. Then take from skillet and place on baking sheet. Top each fillet with slice of cheese and tomato slice. Sprinkle with lemon juice. Bake in preheated oven at 350° for 25 minutes.

Mrs. Harold Gunn, RR #2, Lemmon, S. D. 57638

LAKE TROUT OR DAM TROUT

2 to 3 pounds dressed trout
6 slices bacon
1 thinly sliced onion
1 bay leaf, crushed
3 tbsp. soft butter
2 tbsp. flour
½ c. fine cracker crumbs

Heat oven to 375°.

Sprinkle trout well with salt and pepper. Spread 3 bacon slices along center of pan. Cover with onion; sprinkle with bay leaf; place trout on top. Blend butter with flour and spread on fish. Place trout on top. Sprinkle with crumbs. Place 3 more bacon slices on fish. Bake uncovered 35 to 45 min. or until golden brown and flaky.

Mrs. Edward Ptak, Philip, S. D. 57567

TROUT GERMAN STYLE

trout
chopped onion or onion salt
salt
celery salt

Place several (10-12 inch) trout on wire rack in electric skillet. Pour water over them to partially cover. Sprinkle with onion, salt and celery salt. Cover and cook approximately 10 minutes. Serve immediately with melted butter.

Mrs. Dorothy Williams, 10032 Deadwood Ave.,
Ellsworth AFB, S. D. 57706

BAKED TROUT

3 lb. trout
⅛ tsp. thyme
flour
2 tbsp. butter
3 slices bacon
3 onions
⅛ bottle catsup
1 c. water
⅛ tsp. ginger
paprika
salt and pepper

Salt trout for an hour. Rub in thyme; dust with flour and place in baking dish. Dot the butter over the top; add strips of bacon and sliced onions, catsup, 1 c. water and seasonings. Bake 25 minutes in a slow oven (325°).

Mrs. J. W. Engebretson, Hot Springs, S. D. 57747

BAKED TROUT WITH SOUR CREAM

dressed trout
1 tsp. Worcestershire sauce
1 tsp. prepared mustard
3 tbsp. lemon juice
1½ c. sour cream
1 c. chopped onion
salt and pepper

Line a pan with aluminum foil. Salt and pepper trout. Mix ingredients to make sauce and fill fish. Pour remaining sauce over fish. Bake about 1 hour in a 350° oven. Baste with sauce occasionally while fish bakes. Good for a large trout.

Mrs. Myrtle Warren, 216½ North Broadway, Miller, S. D. 57362

BAKED PADDLEFISH WITH RICE

Fillet fish in medium-sized pieces. Pour over fish, 1 c. lemon juice. Let marinate an hour or more in refrigerator, turning pieces at least once. Drain and put in casserole; cover with the following:

¼ c. chopped onion
2 c. cooked rice, seasoned with chicken bouillon
¼ c. lemon juice
¼ c. water

Bake until fish is tender. Cover with foil during the first half of baking.

Mrs. A. Wesley Evans, 229 Franklin St., Rapid City, S. D. 57701

BAKED STUFFED CARP

1-6 lb. carp.
12 slices bacon

Stuffing:

1 qt. bread cubes
3 tbsp. minced onions
2 tsp. finely crushed sage
¾ tsp. salt
¾ tsp. pepper
¾ c. finely chopped celery
6 tbsp. hot melted butter

Mix stuffing until cubes are moist. Put in stuffing. Heat oven to 500°. Place on aluminum foil in baking dish. Bake until carp browns (about 10 minutes), then take out of oven and cover carp with strips of bacon. Lower heat to 425°. Bake for 35 minutes. Add 5 minutes baking time for each added pound of carp.

Mrs. Leonard Reinke, Box 267, Elkton, S. D. 57026

RED SNAPPER BEAUFORT

6 fillets red snappers or striped bass (about 6 oz. each)
¼ c. minced shallots or green onions
2 c. finely sliced onion (2 large)
1 can (1 lb. 12 oz.) tomatoes, coarsely chopped
1 pound fresh okra, washed and sliced **or** 2 pkgs. frozen okra thawed
salt and pepper
melted butter or margarine

Heat oven to 400°. Butter a shallow baking pan just large enough to hold the fillets. Fold the fillets, if desired. Arrange shallots or green onions, onions, tomatoes and okra on bottom of pan. Place fillets over vegetables. Brush with melted butter or margarine. Bake 10-15 minutes or until fish flakes easily. Remove fillets with large slotted spatula. Keep warm. Transfer vegetables and juice to saucepan. Bring to boiling point and simmer 5 minutes. Correct seasoning to taste. Arrange vegetables in center of serving platter. Place fillets over vegetables. Pour remaining juice over fish.
Makes servings for six.

Mrs. Art Pavin, 338 St. Anne E., Rapid City, S. D. 57701

OVEN FRIED FISH

8 fillet of fish or pieces of fish
1 stick of margarine or butter
1 egg
1 cup bread crumbs (fine) or cracker crumbs
salt and pepper

Heat oven to 375° and put butter in pan in oven. Watch so it doesn't burn. Dip fish in beaten egg then in crumbs to coat well. Place in buttered pan. Turn to coat evenly. Season to taste. Bake 20-25 minutes.

Mrs. August Kaldowske, 1202 E. 7th St., Sioux Falls, S. D. 57103

STUFFED FRIED FISH

fish
½ cup rice
butter
1 large onion, chopped
¼ cup tomato sauce
cracker crumbs

Boil rice in salted water until done. Melt part of the butter in a pan and fry onion. Mix with the cooked rice and tomato sauce. This will be the stuffing for the fish.

Clean fish. Cut off the head, and wash fish thoroughly inside. Stuff the fish with the filling; roll in cracker crumbs and fry in butter.

Hilda Heyne, 1036 E. Ohio, Rapid City, S. D. 57701

DEEP FRIED LAKE TROUT

12 lake trout
seasoned flour
2 eggs
4 tbsp. water
cracker crumbs, finely crushed
deep fat for frying

Clean and chill medium-sized lake trout. Use chore girl to remove scales. Leave whole unless they are over 9" in length. Otherwise split lengthwise. Drain well. Beat eggs with water. First: roll trout in seasoned flour. Second: dip trout in egg mixture. Third: roll in cracker crumbs. Fry until brown in oil 375° about 5-7 minutes. Serve with potato salad and a hot buttered vegetable.

Mrs. Roy G. Anderson, Box 101, Irene, S. D. 57037

TROUT AMANDINE

1 to 1½ lb. trout
2 eggs, beaten
salt and black pepper
flour
1 c. salad oil
toasted shredded almonds
¼ c. butter
¼ tsp. salt
¼ tsp. white pepper
1 tsp. finely chopped parsley
½ clove garlic, finely chopped

Remove skin from trout with sharp knife. Cut out 2 boneless fillets. Dip in eggs; season with salt and pepper. Dredge in flour. Heat oil in skillet; saute fish until brown, turning once. Place on warm platter, sprinkle with almonds. Melt butter, add salt, white pepper, parsley and garlic. Pour over fillets, serve.

Mrs. Calvin Andersen, 709 Vine Street, Hudson, Wisconsin 54016

NORTHERN PIKE

4 fillets of northern pike (12-18 inches long)
2 c. pancake mix
1 king-size bottle 7-Up
deep fat for frying

Cut fillets into 1 inch square pieces. Take a pair of pliers and remove all bones from these pieces. "This is a tedious chore but the results are well worth it." After making sure all bones are removed, add enough 7-Up to the pancake mix to make a sticky batter. Dip the cut-up and boned pieces of fish into the batter and then into a deep fat fryer when fat is at 350°. Fry until pancake batter is a golden brown all over. Serve with a cocktail sauce, soda crackers, butter and a favorite cold beverage.

Mr. Lyle Johnson, Brandon, S. D. 57005

PAN FRIED WHITE BASS

6 small white bass
1 c. buttermilk
juice of one lemon
½ c. corn meal
½ c. instant mashed potatoes
¼ tsp. pepper
½ tsp. salt
2 c. shortening

Soak fish overnight in buttermilk and lemon juice. Roll fish in a mixture of corn meal and mashed potato flakes, plus salt and pepper. Heat shortening until piping hot. Add fish and cook until brown—approximately 8 to 10 minutes on each side.
These fish are delicious fried!

Skeeter Proctor, Oklahoma Game and Fish Dept.

FISH FRIED

Dip fish in salted flour, and fry in ½ butter and ½ shortening until golden brown and cooked through. Good for bullheads and catfish.

Mrs. Louis J. Peterson, 23 S.E. 80th, Portland, Oregon 97215

PADDLEFISH FRITTERS

Poach fish about ten minutes, or until skin and bones can be removed. (Sturgeon can also be used.)

2 c. fish flesh
4 crushed soda crackers, rolled very fine
2 eggs, slightly beaten
½ tsp. salt
⅛ tsp. pepper
½ tsp. Mei Yen powder
dash of lemon juice

Combine all ingredients. Drop from tablespoon onto hot griddle. Fry over medium heat. Garnish with parsley and serve with tartar sauce.

Karl M. Rottluff, M.D., Box 1822, Sante Fe, New Mexico 87501

PLYMOUTH STEW

6 slices salt pork, partially cooked
2 med. fillets of sole, cut in 6 inch strips
salt and pepper
1 onion, chopped fine
12 crackers
milk
1 c. white wine
1 c. water
1 tbsp. butter
2 tbsp. flour

Cover bottom of Dutch oven with salt pork slices. Lay fish over this and sprinkle with salt and pepper. Spread chopped onion over this. Cover with crackers soaked in milk. Pour over all, wine and water. Simmer for about 1 hour. Remove fish and pork to platter. Thicken liquid with butter and flour. Pour over fish and serve. Serves 6.

Mrs. Kermit Karst, 514 Belmont Drive, Rapid City, S. D. 57701

PADDLEFISH

paddlefish strips
flour
1 egg
2 tbsp. water
salt and pepper
cracker crumbs

Cut white meat off paddlefish in strips ½ inch by 1 inch and 4-5 inches long. Roll in white flour. Dip in egg, water, salt and pepper beaten together. Coat with cracker crumbs. Fry in deep fat, till golden brown. Drain on paper towels.

Variation:

For a different coating for fish or meat frying, mix equal parts of white flour, cornmeal and instant non-fat milk powder.

Mrs. John Voeltz, Box 100, RR #2, Howard, S. D. 57349

BARBECUED FISH

Clean perch or bass and fillet. Season with salt and pepper. Lay in a baking dish. Make sauce of:

3 tbsp. fat
2 tbsp. minced onion
2 tbsp. vinegar
salt and pepper
1 small clove garlic, sliced
2 tbsp. brown sugar
⅓ bottle catsup

Lightly brown onion and garlic in fat. Add rest of ingredients and heat well. Pour over fish and bake until fish is done. (About 30 min. at 350°)

Mrs. Myrtle Warren, 216½ North Broadway, Miller, S. D. 57362

POACHED WALLEYE

3 lbs. walleye (fresh)
2 tsp. salt
1 tsp. pepper
4 tbsp. water
3 tbsp. butter
4 tbsp. lemon juice
1 small onion, minced
1 sprig parsley, minced

Fillet fish, rub in salt and pepper. Drizzle lemon juice over fillets. Then spread with butter. Sprinkle on onion and parsley. Add water, wrap in foil and place over medium barbecue coals for 20 minutes. Turn occasionally.

Mrs. J. J. Rath, Box "F", Leola, S. D. 57456

PRESSURE COOKED SEA PERCH

2 lbs. perch, scaled and cleaned
2 tbsp. fat
salt and pepper
½ c. water in cooker with rack

Heat cooker and add fat. Brown perch. Place rack under perch. Add water. Place cover on cooker. Allow steam to flow from vent pipe to release air. Place indicator weight on vent pipe. Cook 10 minutes with stem at COOK position. Cool cooker at once.

Mrs. Ed Markus, Corsica, S. D. 57328

FISH CHOWDER

1 (4 lb.) trout or equivalent
2 c. celery, cut fine
1 medium onion, cut fine
1 large can tomatoes
1 can consomme
1 can peas or 1 pkg. frozen corn
2 tbsp. creamed corn, optional
¼ tsp. pepper, season to taste
2 tsp. salt, or season to taste
½ pint cream

Skin fish; cut meat into small pieces; add celery and onion. Cover with water; simmer 10 min. Add tomatoes, consomme, peas, corn, and season. Simmer 45 minutes. Just before serving add cream. Serve with green salad and corn bread. Serves 4.

Mrs. Dave Robin, PO Box #463, Upton, Wyoming 82730

FISH CHOWDER

3 slices salt pork or bacon, cut fine
1 sliced onion
2 tbsp. celery, chopped
2 tbsp. green pepper, chopped
6 medium potatoes, cut in cubes
1 qt. fish flakes
2 c. water
4 c. milk
1 tbsp. butter
1 tbsp. salt
1 tbsp. thyme

Fry out salt pork or bacon; add onion, celery and pepper. Cook carefully until a light brown. Parboil potatoes and brown in fat. Add chopped fish and water; cook ten minutes. Add milk and butter; season and serve. (Any kind of fish can be used.)

Mrs. J. W. Engebretson, Hot Springs, S. D. 57747

Variation:
Two diced carrots can be added with the potatoes. A bouillon cube can also be dissolved in the 2 c. water to add flavor.

Mrs. A. Wesley Evans, 229 Franklin St., Rapid City, S. D. 57701

SIMPLE FISH CHOWDER

2 lbs. fish
6 slices bacon, diced
2 small onions, chopped
2 tbsp. salt
dash of pepper
1 qt. milk

Simmer fish in slightly salted water until meat can be separated from bones easily. Save water but drain off bits of skin, bone, etc. Fry bacon and onion together until browned. Add potatoes to water in which fish was cooked, plus salt and pepper. When potatoes are done, add fish, bacon, onions and milk. Bring to boil but don't let it boil! Use minimum amount of water for cooking fish and potatoes. Serves 6.

Mrs. Kermit Karst, 514 Belmont Drive, Rapid City, S. D. 57701

Note: Almost any fish can be used, small trout are delicious. Tomatoes can be added if desired.

FISH EGG SOUP

eggs from yellow perch
1 c. water
¼ tsp. salt
dash pepper
2 c. whole milk
2 tbsp. butter

Save and cut in pieces 10 eggs from yellow perch. Add water, salt and a dash of pepper. Boil together 10 minutes. Add milk and butter. Bring to boil. Serve hot.

Mrs. John Voeltz, Box 100 RR#2, Howard, S. D. 57349

TROUT CHOWDER

trout
2 medium potatoes
1 onion, chopped
1 can evaporated milk
1 can corn
¼ lb. butter
salt and pepper

Dice potatoes and boil until about half done. Place trout in kettle of boiling water to cover. Boil until meat loosens from bones. Remove bones and place meat back in the water in which it has been boiled. Add chopped onions to season, evaporated milk, corn, butter, salt and pepper, and the half-cooked potatoes. Cook slowly ten minutes and serve.

Hilda Heyne, 1036 E. Ohio, Rapid City, S. D. 57701

CATFISH BALLS

2 c. flaked fish
2 c. mashed potatoes
1 egg
salt and pepper
deep-fat frying oil

Bake or steam catfish. Best way is with a pressure cooker. Remove fish from bones and flake. Blend flaked fish, mashed potatoes, egg, salt and pepper to taste. Shape in balls and deep fry until golden brown.

Mrs. Dave Robin, PO Box #463, Upton, Wyoming 82730

PICKLED FISH

Fillet and cut in strips 1 inch wide.
Fill quart jars ¾ full, do not pack.
Add:

3 tbsp. salt
¼ c. sugar
2 tsp. pickling spice
1 medium onion, diced

Fill remainder of jar with white vinegar. Refrigerate 4 days and it's ready to eat.

Mrs. Russel Jacobs, Box 67, Roslyn, S. D. 57261

PICKLED FISH

Fillet and skin any fish you care to use. Be sure to remove the rib cages. Now cut them into about 1½ inch square chunks or ¼ to 1 inch strips. Fill a qt. jar about ¾ full of these sliced fillets plus 1 diced onion. Pack very loosely. Add the following:

2 tbsp. salt
7 tbsp. sugar
2 tsp. whole mixed pickling spice
1½ oz. dry white wine
apple cider vinegar

Fill the jar with wine and vinegar right to the top. Now shake the jar to thoroughly mix the ingredients. Refrigerate for four days and they're ready to eat. During the four days shake the jar from time to time.

Note: If you like it sweeter, add a bit more sugar, but don't change the salt content. If you like a more vinegar taste leave the wine out, as all this does is cut the vinegar a bit. Optional, 1 red pepper and/or clove garlic.

Mrs. Fred M. Rosin, Jr.

CANNED LAKE TROUT

fillet of trout
2 tsp. salt
2 tsp. catsup
2 tsp. vinegar

Fillet the trout (one side usually fills 1 pt. jar). Pack in a pint jar and add salt, catsup and vinegar. Seal jars and pressure cook at 10 lb. pressure for 80 min.

Better than frozen trout as it can be kept indefinitely and doesn't dry out. The trout tastes like salmon and the bones can be eaten too.

Mrs. L. Ramsdell, 808 6th Ave. W., Lemmon, S. D. 57638

CANNED TROUT

Clean and scale trout. Cut in pieces. Put in pint fruit jars. Pack smaller pieces in center and add:

1 tsp. butter
½ tsp. salt
1 tbsp. vinegar

Cook in pressure cooker 10 lb. for 100 minutes.

Mrs. Rowena Rachetts, Box 654, Spearfish, S. D. 57783

PICKLED BULLHEADS

bullheads
4 med. onions
5 to 6 bay leaves
1 tbsp. whole pickling spice
2 c. vinegar
1½ c. water
1 tbsp. salt
pepper

Cut up onions; put on bottom of small roaster; add bay leaves and whole pickling spice. Lay skinned bullheads over this close together. May use more than one layer. Cover with a solution of 2 cups vinegar to 1½ cups water and 1 tbsp. salt and pepper. Cover and boil slowly till fish are cooked. Cool in roaster till cold. Serve cold.

Mrs. John Voeltz, Box 100, RR #2, Howard, S. D. 57349

Prairie Sea Food

TO PREPARE A TURTLE

First cut off the head and feet and turn it upside down nailing the tail to a board. Use a very sharp thin knife and cut the skin from around the back shell. Cut off the belly plate; skin the neck and tail and other skin off. Remove the internal organs. Also remove the two tenderloin strips along the back. Cut the fatty tissue away and wash the turtle meat in cold water and you are ready to cook it. It has a taste almost like chicken.

TURTLE STEAKS

Slice turtle meat in slices, dip in flour and fry in hot fat as you would fry round steak or chicken.

**Mrs. George D. Wallenstein, 622 North Sherman Ave.,
Sioux Falls, S. D. 57103**

MOSS BACK TURTLE

Cut the head off, turn upside down so it will bleed well, almost an hour. Skin, remove the flesh from the shell. Cut meat in medium pieces, soak in salt water, 1 cup to a gallon of water, about an hour. Season with salt and pepper. Fry in hot lard until brown and well done. Turn often. Serve with hot baking powder biscuits, mashed potatoes and apple pie.

**Mrs. A. H. Waters, RR #1, 158 Coldbrook Road,
Hot Springs, S. D. 57747**

TURTLE SOUP

3 lbs. turtle meat, cut small
4 tbsp. fat
4 tbsp. flour
1 c. tomatoes
1 tbsp. salt
¼ clove garlic, minced fine
4 qts. stock and water
1 lump sugar
2 bay leaves
2 sprigs parsley
6 cloves
½ tsp. mace
2 tbsp. lemon juice

Parboil meat for 10 minutes; save water for stock. Fry meat in fat. Remove meat from pan and brown the flour. Add tomatoes, salt and garlic. Add remaining ingredients and bring to a boil. Add turtle meat. Cook three hours; strain if desired.

Mrs. Dave Robin, PO Box #463, Upton, Wyoming 82730

TURTLE STEW

2¼ c. turtle meat, cut in 1 inch cubes
4 tbsp. margarine
1 medium onion, sliced
2 c. diced celery
3 med. potatoes, peeled and diced
3 med. carrots, peeled and diced
1 c. fresh lima beans
1 c. tomatoes
½ c. parsley
salt and pepper

Place onion, lima beans, celery in Dutch oven and cover with water. Bring to boil and simmer 30 minutes. In meantime, saute the turtle meat in margarine in skillet till brown on all sides. Add meat, margarine, potatoes, carrots, tomatoes, parsley, salt and pepper to the vegetables in Dutch oven. Simmer for 45 minutes or till all vegetables are tender.
Serves 6.

Mrs. Kermit Karst, 514 Belmont Drive, Rapid City, S. D. 57701

FRIED TURTLE

1 med. sized turtle
1 tsp. salt
½ tsp. pepper
2 bay leaves
seasoned flour
fat or butter

Clean and disjoint the turtle into medium-sized pieces. Place in a stewing kettle with salt, pepper and bay leaves. Add water to cover meat, and boil for 15 min. Let turtle cool in its broth. Drain well. Dust with seasoned flour and fry in a heavy skillet, as you would chicken, until it is tender and golden brown. If you wish, make a cream gravy from the residue in the skillet.

Mrs. Jerome Renz, 801 E. Oakland St., Rapid City, S. D. 57701

SNAPPING TURTLE SOUP

One large snapping turtle

Use ax to chop off head and with shell upside down use ax to remove top from bottom. Using a very sharp knife skin out legs, neck, and tail. Cook in water slowly as rapid cooking toughens the meat. Simmer about 3 hrs. Remove meat from bones and now make your favorite home made vegetable soup. Use the heart and liver in the soup.

Mrs. Elmer Rauscher, 512 North Madison, Pierre, S. D. 57501

TURTLE PIE

1½ c. turtle meat cut in cubes
1 onion, diced
3 tbsp. butter
3 tbsp. flour
1½ c. water

Brown the turtle meat in butter, add diced onion and salt and pepper to taste. Add the water and let simmer for about an hour then remove it from the water and put in a greased casserole. Make a thin flour paste and add it to the turtle meat. Make a baking powder biscuit dough and cover the casserole with it. Bake in hot oven until the biscuits are brown.

Mrs. George D. Wallenstein, 622 North Sherman Ave., Sioux Falls, S. D. 57103

TURTLE GOULASH

1½ lbs. turtle meat cut in cubes
1 onion, diced
3 tbsp. butter
8 carrots, sliced
4 potatoes, sliced
2 sprigs parsley
1½ tsp. salt
dash of pepper
3 tbsp. flour

Brown meat and onion in butter. Salt and pepper and cover with one cup water and let simmer for one hour or until tender. Add the vegetables about one half hour before serving. After the vegetables are cooked add flour paste to thicken the goulash.
This is really good cooked in an iron kettle over an outdoor fire.

Mrs. George D. Wallenstein, 622 North Sherman Ave., Sioux Falls, S. D. 57103

TURTLE SOUP

3 lbs. turtle meat
3½ qts. water
2 med. onions, finely chopped
1 stalk celery, finely chopped
¼ bay leaf
2 sprigs parsley
6 cloves
1 tsp. sugar
1 c. canned tomatoes
1 tbsp. salt
½ tsp. whole black peppers
3 tbsp. butter

Wipe meat clean with damp cloth. Cut meat from bones and add bones and gristle to water in a kettle. Add the remaining ingredients except butter; heat to boiling; reduce heat and simmer covered for 1 hour. Strain and discard vegetables and bones. Meanwhile cut turtle meat in small cubes, about ¼" and brown slowly in the butter until cubes are golden brown on all sides. Add browned meat and any remaining drippings to the strained broth; heat to boiling; reduce heat and simmer for 20-30 min. until a rich flavor is developed in broth and the turtle meat is done. Do not overcook. Add more salt and pepper if needed. Serve piping hot.
Serves 8-10.

Mrs. Chuck Callahan, 1701 Tepee St., Rapid City, S. D. 57701

TURTLE SOUP

1½ qts. strained chicken broth
1 lb. turtle meat (without bones or gristle)
3 tsp. chicken fat or butter
1 med. onion, chopped
salt and pepper to taste
1 tsp. chopped parsley
5 to 6 thin slices lemon

Prepare a richly flavored chicken broth seasoned only with salt. Strain. Cut turtle meat into small pieces. Brown slowly in the chicken fat (or butter). Add onion and saute slowly over medium heat until onion is soft and yellow. Add turtle, onion, seasoning and any fat to chicken broth; heat to boiling; reduce heat and simmer gently for 10 min. Serve with a sprinkling of parsley on each bowl of soup and a paper-thin slice of lemon floated on top.
5-6 servings.

Mrs. Chuck Callahan, 1701 Tepee St., Rapid City, S. D. 57701

TURTLE SOUP

1 turtle
1 onion, diced
½ c. peas
1 tbsp. pearl barley
1 carrot, diced
½ bunch celery, diced
1 c. tomatoes, diced or sauce
salt and pepper
parsley to taste

Wash the turtle, cut the skin from under shell, skin legs and neck and remove all fat. Cut up and wash. Cook 3 hours in 4 qts. water. When tender lift out meat and add vegetables. Cook vegetables until tender. Chop meat and put in soup.

Mrs. J. W. Engebretson, Hot Springs, S. D. 57747

TURTLE SOUP

turtle meat
½ to ¾ c. pearl barley
2 cans Veg-All (including juice)
½ bag wide noodles
2 small onions, chopped
½ lb. butter

Cover turtle meat with water, adding more water to meat if needed when cooking. Boil; skim and then add the pearl barley. Cook this until done. Remove meat. Put in Veg-All, noodles and onions. Cook until noodles are tender. Just before serving add meat which has been browned in the butter. Start this in the afternoon to serve at night.

Mrs. Leonard Reinke, Box 267, Elkton, S. D. 57026

TURTLE SOUP

1½ c. diced fresh turtle meat
2 qt. beef stock
1 bay leaf
1½ tbsp. lemon juice
1 clove mace
3 drops Tabasco sauce
1 hard-cooked egg white diced fine
salt and pepper
⅓ c. sherry wine

Combine turtle meat, beef stock, bay leaf, mace, lemon juice and Tabasco sauce. Bring to boiling point and cook until turtle meat is tender. Remove bay leaf and mace, add egg white and season with salt and pepper. Add sherry wine after removing soup from heat. Serves 8.

Mrs. Edwin Syrovatka, 119 Trinidad, Naples, Florida 33940

TURTLE STEW

1 qt. cooked turtle meat
broth
3 to 4 med. potatoes chunked
2 med. onions, diced
1 small can corn
2 No. 3 cans tomatoes
salt and pepper
2 tbsp. butter

Take about a qt. of the pressure-cooked turtle chunks and use enough broth to cook the vegetables; add potatoes, onion, corn, tomatoes, seasonings and butter. Bring to boil; lower heat and simmer until vegetables are tender.

Mrs. Dave Robin, PO Box 463, Upton, Wyoming 82730

CRAYFISH RECIPE

crayfish (Secure a good supply of crayfish—allow one pound live weight per person)
2 bay leaves
1 tsp. caraway seed, if you have it
¼ c. salt

Place crayfish in a tub of clean water for 10-12 hours. Next use a large kettle, filling it with water; add bay leaves, caraway seed and salt. Bring to a boil and drop in live crayfish. Cook until crayfish turns bright red (6-10 min.) Drain off water and allow to cool. Break off tails, peel, removing gall cysts and digestive tract. As you get the touch, you can accomplish this in a single jerk. Crayfish can now be either prepared in a cocktail or fried.

Fried crayfish tails:

1 qt. crayfish tails, boiled and cleaned
1 egg
1½ c. milk
salt and pepper
flour or corn meal
cooking oil

Break egg into a bowl, add milk, salt, pepper and mix thoroughly. Dip tails into egg mixture, dust with flour or corn meal and drop into deep fat (375°) and cook until golden brown. Serve as you would shrimp with sliced lemon and your favorite sauce.

FROG LEGS

24 med. frog legs
seasoned flour
oil
2 tbsp. butter
1 c. chopped mushrooms
¼ c. chopped shallots (onions)
½ c. chopped parsley
salt and pepper
¼ c. dry white wine

Skin frog legs and role them in seasoned flour and fry in hot oil until golden brown. In another skillet, melt butter; add mushrooms, shallots and parsley. Saute until just done and season with salt and pepper. Place frog legs on very hot serving plate. Cover with mushroom mixture and pour wine over the top.

Mrs. George D. Wallenstein, 622 North Sherman, Sioux Falls, S. D. 57103

BREADED FROG LEGS

Frog legs (hind quarters only) are quite delicious. The skin can be turned over and skinned off like a glove.

6 frog legs, skinned
1 egg
lemon juice
salt and pepper
fine bread crumbs

Wash legs in cold water; dry well on a towel. Season with salt, pepper and lemon juice. Dip in beaten egg then in fine bread crumbs. Fry in deep hot fat for 2-3 minutes or until brown.
Serve with tartar sauce.

Mrs. George D. Wallenstein, 622 N. Sherman, Sioux Falls, S. D. 57103

MAINE LOBSTER STEW

4 c. milk
1 sliced onion
1 c. diced fresh lobster
3 tbsp. butter
1 tsp. salt
⅛ tsp. paprika
2 tbsp. chopped parsley

Scald milk with onion. Remove onion and add remaining ingredients. Heat to boiling point and serve immediately.
Serves 4.

Mrs. Edwin Syrovatka, 119 Trinidad, Naples, Florida 33940

FROG LEGS

Cut legs off just above the hips and remove the skin. Place the legs in a strong salt solution for several hours. Make a batter of the yolks of eggs and cracker crumbs. Wipe frog legs dry, dip in batter and fry brown in deep fat.

Hilda Heyne, 1036 E. Ohio, Rapid City, S. D. 57701

CRAYFISH ETOUFEE

Proportions:

Crayfish (boiled and peeled) ½ lb./person
¼ lb. crayfish fat/2 lb. crayfish
½ lb. butter/2 lb. crayfish
2 lb. crayfish
2 large onions, chopped
3 bell peppers, chopped
1 stalk celery, chopped
parsley, chopped
2 whole garlic, chopped
red and black pepper
salt

Melt butter in large heavy roaster or Dutch oven and add chopped vegetables. Allow to saute 20-30 minutes or until cooked down. As vegetables near completion add crayfish fat. Add crayfish, along with chopped garlic, red and black pepper and salt to taste. Should use enough red pepper to "incite" the palate, but don't get carried away. Cook at med. boil for 30 minutes. Add enough water to achieve desired thickness. Upon completion, should resemble a thick soup.

Serve with boiled rice, tossed salad and hot French bread seasoned with butter and garlic salt.

Art Brazda, Flyway Biologist, U.S. Fish and Wildlife Service

Fowl

FRIED PHEASANT AND ONIONS

pheasant breasts
3 large onions
frying shortening
seasoned flour or cracker meal
salt and pepper
butter

Steak out the breasts (same for ducks including the legs.) Have a fairly hot fire going with an ample amount of shortening. Take three fairly large onions and slice them. When the shortening gets hot put the onions in and let them cook as long as the individuals would like (some like them real crisp and some like them black).
In the meantime, take the breasts of the pheasants; cut them into either two or three pieces; pound them with the back edge of a knife to break down the outside tissues; roll them in flour or cracker meal; salt and pepper and put them in the frying pan. Cover with the onions turning them twice with ample salt, pepper and butter added. The pan should be covered, cook just long enough so that they are tender and cooked through. Do not cook too long so they get tough. Serve the onions and pheasant together.

PHEASANT WITH WILD RICE DRESSING

2 pheasants
1 c. wild rice cooked in 1 qt. water with 1 tsp. salt for 40 min. Drain off unabsorbed water and dry rice by spreading on towel. To the rice add:

2 tbsp. minced onion
2 tbsp. minced green pepper
2 tbsp. minced celery
1 4 oz. can chopped mushrooms, drained
¼ tsp. pepper
¼ lb. butter, melted
4 slices bacon

Wipe birds inside and out with a damp cloth. Stuff with wild rice dressing. Place breast side up on rack in roasting pan. Lay 2 slices of bacon over each breast. Roast in slow oven at 325° until tender. (About 2½ hrs.) Baste frequently with melted butter and pan drippings.
Serves 4-6.

Mrs. Calvin Andersen, 708 Vine St., Hudson, Wisconsin 54016

FRIED PHEASANT

pheasant, cut up
1 egg, beaten
1 c. milk
¼ c. instant potatoes
¼ c. corn meal
¼ c. flour
peanut oil

Add milk to beaten egg. Dip cut up pheasant in the milk mixture and coat with a mixture of instant potatoes, corn meal and flour. Brown in peanut oil (peanut oil has a low burning point.) Lower heat and steam done. An electric fry pan works well for this recipe.

Mrs. Arthur Birkeland, Pierpont, S. D. 57468

BAKED PHEASANT WITH BREAD DRESSING

Leave pheasant whole. When ready to fix, place bird in greased roaster and brush with melted butter and sprinkle with salt inside and out. Then make the following dressing:

4 c. soft bread crumbs
1 tsp. poultry seasoning
2 small stalks of celery, cut fine
2 tbsp. finely chopped onion
¼ tsp. salt
pepper to season
pheasant giblets
⅔ c. warm water or stock in which giblets have been cooked

Cook giblets in water until almost tender. Drain and reserve liquid. Combine all ingredients for dressing and add chopped giblets and stock. Lightly stuff pheasant with dressing. Make a cup of aluminum foil and poke holes in bottom. Fill with remaining dressing and put beside the pheasant in roaster. Cover and bake in oven at 325° for 3 hrs. or until very well done.

Mrs. Ed Hansen, Larchwood, Iowa 51241

Variation:

After stuffing the pheasant with the dressing recipe given above or your own favorite dressing, place in a roaster and cover the bird with a cloth soaked in margarine. This will keep it moist. Add 1 c. water in the bottom of the roaster and cover. Bake 2 hrs. or until well done. Make a gravy from the drippings.

Mrs. Louis J. Peterson, 23 S. E. 80th, Portland, Oregon 97215

BATTER-FRIED PHEASANT

2 eggs
2 tbsp. water

Beat together well and set in refrigerator until ready to use. It should be gooey. (about 1 hr.)

flour
fine bread crumbs (1 slice)
cooking oil
1 can mushroom soup
½ can water

Dip pheasant pieces into egg batter and roll in flour. Dip in egg batter again, roll in fine bread crumbs. Cover pheasant well with the crumbs. (A blender works nicely for making the bread crumbs.) Refrigerate pheasant pieces for two hours. Heat ½" cooking oil to 350-375°. (Be sure the oil is hot before adding the pheasant.) Put pieces in grease, brown well turning only once. Salt pieces. Put pieces in casserole and pour mushroom soup diluted with water over pheasant. Cover tightly and bake in oven 350° for 50 to 60 min.

Mrs. Ray Konechne, RR #2, Kimball, S. D. 57355

PHEASANT STEAKS

Cut the entire breast of a pheasant in 2 pieces. Pound real well. Cut out as much bone as possible. Pat some seasoned flour into the 2 parts and fry quickly in a skillet over moderate heat. Turn just as you would a steak and brown both sides well. Two of the best flavored steaks ever!

Then take all the rest—bones from steaks—and make soup. Cook long and slow. Add a few carrots, an onion, salt and even a little quick-cooking rice or some potatoes.

Mrs. Sig Simonson, 813 Pine St., Yankton, S. D. 57078

Variation:

Follow directions for steaks as given above with the addition of a very small piece of bay leaf which is put on each piece. The rest of the pieces can be cooked in a pressure cooker until tender. Remove the meat from the bones and grind for sandwich filling. If you like onion, grind a little with the meat. The stock can be used for soup. Or, if you prefer, use the pieces of meat in a casserole dish with rice or noodles and cream of mushroom soup.

Artie J. Calhoon, 127 St. Joe St., Rapid City, S. D. 57701

BAKED PHEASANT IN MUSHROOM SAUCE

2 pheasants, cut-up
1 c. flour
2 tsp. salt
½ tsp. pepper
6 tbsp. bacon fat

Sauce:

1 can mushroom soup
½ c. milk
1 med. onion, sliced

Coat pheasants with a mixture of flour, salt and pepper. In skillet lightly brown pheasant in bacon grease. Remove from skillet, put in baking casserole and cover with soup, milk and onion slices. Bake for 1 hr. at 275° or until desired doneness.
Note: A couple of slices of cheeese over the top adds elegance.

Note: Brown pheasant as above and remove from skillet. Put in baking casserole to which 1½ to 2 c. dry red wine has been added. Cook at 275°, basting occasionally with wine until desired doneness.

Mrs. Nancy Brady, Mt. Vernon, S. D. 57363

Variation:

Add a dash of cinnamon to flour mixture, brown in oil, place in a flat baking dish. Pour over a sauce made of 1 can of cream of mushroom soup and ¾ c. cream or canned milk. Bake without covering in a 300° oven for 30 min.

Mrs. Roy G. Anderson, Box 101, Irene, S. D. 57037

Variation:

After browning floured pieces of pheasant, place in a baking dish and cover with 1 can mushroom soup. Add a little water and bake until tender at 350°.

Rose Paulsen, RR #1, Miller, S. D. 57362

PHEASANT AND WILD RICE

1 c. raw wild rice
1 can cream of chicken soup
1 can cream of mushroom soup
1 can mushroom stems and pieces
2½ c. water
water chestnuts, if desired
2 pheasants, cut up, floured and browned
1 pkg. Lipton onion soup mix

Mix rice, canned soups, water, mushrooms and chestnuts if desired, in a casserole. Add pheasant. Sprinkle dry onion soup over. Cover lightly with foil. Bake for 3 hrs. at 300°.

Mrs. J. J. Rath, Box "F", Leola, S. D. 57456

SMOTHERED PHEASANT

pheasant, cut in serving pieces
½ c. flour
1 tsp. salt
dash pepper
paprika
¼ c. shortening
½ c. liquid (water, light cream or cream of mushroom soup mixed with milk)

Mix the flour and seasonings in a paper or plastic bag. Shake the cut-up pheasant, a piece or two at a time, in the bag. Add the pheasant to the hot fat and brown well on each side. Reduce heat to simmer. Add liquid. Cover and continue cooking for 1 hr. or until tender. May add more liquid if needed, during the cooking period.

Clara W. Johnson, Home Economics Agent, Watertown, S. D. 57201
Mrs. Daniel K. Hoffman, Longlake, S. D. 57457

Variation:

Instead of light cream add 1 chopped green pepper and just before serving add 1 c. sour cream.

Miss Evelyn Peterson, RR #2, Emery, S. D. 57332

SMOTHERED PHEASANT IN MUSHROOM SAUCE

3 to 4 lbs. pheasants, cut-up
¼ c. flour
¼ c. melted butter
1 large can evaporated milk
1 (10½ oz.) can cream of mushroom soup
1 c. grated processed cheese
¾ tsp. salt
⅛ tsp. pepper
6 to 8 small cooked onions
¼ lb. sliced mushrooms

Coat pheasant pieces with flour. Place pieces in a single layer in the melted butter in a shallow baking dish. Bake uncovered in a 425° oven for 30 min. Turn pheasant, bake for 15 min. more. Pour off excess fat. Mix milk, soup, cheese, salt and pepper together. Add onions and mushrooms to pheasant. Pour evaporated milk mixture over pheasant. Cover dish with aluminum foil. Reduce oven to 325°. Bake 15 to 20 min.
Serves 6 to 8.

Mrs. Oliver Carlson, Seneca, S. D. 57473

SCALLOPED PHEASANT

1 pheasant, steamed until tender.
Drain and save the broth.

Gravy:
1 qt. liquid (broth)
5 tbsp. flour
1 tsp. salt
¼ tsp. pepper

Dressing:
1½ qts. bread crumbs
¾ c. melted butter
1½ tsp. sage
¾ tsp. salt
¼ c. liquid or broth
2 tbsp. chopped onion

Make gravy using broth, flour, salt and pepper. Make dressing of bread crumbs, melted butter, sage, salt, liquid and onion. Cube the cooked pheasant and toss lightly with dressing. Place in a greased baking dish and pour gravy over top. Bake in 350° oven for 30 min. or until brown. Freezes well.
Serves 6.

Mrs. Myrtle Warren, 216½ North Broadway, Miller, S. D. 57362

SCALLOPED PHEASANT

pheasant
1 tsp. salt
water to almost cover meat
1 c. bread crumbs
2 tbsp. melted butter

Cut up a pheasant and cook until tender. Pour off and save broth. Remove bones and dice pheasant. Make a gravy of the broth, using ½ broth and ½ whole milk. Thicken slightly. Season to taste. Moisten bread crumbs in melted butter. In greased casserole, place alternate layers of diced pheasant, gravy and crumbs. Bake at 350° until thoroughly heated, and the top crumbs are brown.
Serves 3 to 4.

Mrs. Virginia Uresk, 3327 W. Rapid, Rapid City, S. D. 57701

GOLDEN PHEASANT CASSEROLE

1 pheasant, dressed and washed in cool salt water.
Cut in serving pieces. (8 or 10)

Roll pheasant pieces in flour, seasoned with salt and pepper. Using half butter and half bacon drippings in a heavy skillet, fry the pieces until golden brown on all sides. Place pheasants in a deep casserole. Then add a layer of thickly sliced potatoes, a layer of onion slices and a layer of sliced carrots.

Combine 1 can of cream of mushroom soup and 1 c. sour cream, 1 tbsp. Worcestershire sauce and 1½ c. water and pour this over the vegetables. Cover casserole and bake at 325° until all vegetables are tender (about 1½ hrs.) Remove cover and top with baking powder biscuits (use your own recipe or packaged biscuits from dairy case). Continue baking until biscuits are brown.

Mrs. Therman W. Patzlaff, West View Farm, Alexandria, S. D. 57311

PHEASANT IN CREAM WITH VEGETABLES

Roll pieces of pheasant in flour and brown in hot grease. (Use part butter for flavor) Place in casserole, add layer of sliced potatoes, layer of sliced onion, and layer of halved carrots. Cover with cream, sweet or sour. Bake 300° oven until all vegetables are tender. (About 1½ hrs.)

Mrs. Rudy Scholl, RR #1, Box 64, Madison, S. D. 57042

PHEASANT

1 pheasant, cut-up
½ c. fat
½ c. flour
salt and pepper
1 med. onion, sliced (optional)
1 c. light cream

Roll pheasant in seasoned flour. Brown slowly in hot fat—turning once. Put in baking dish and cover with onion slices and light cream. Cover tightly with lid and roast at 300° for 1 hour.

Mrs. Bill Seney, 1028 W. Clark, Vermillion, S. D. 57069

EASY PHEASANT BREASTS SUPREME

6 pheasant breasts, halved and skinned
1 can cream of mushroom soup
1 can cream of chicken soup
1 med. onion, sliced into rings

Place pheasant in saucepan with enough water to cover, boil uncovered for 1 hr. and 30 min. Place pheasant into a 2 qt. casserole, cover with soups and onion rings. Bake covered at 350° for 2 hrs. Yield 4 servings.

Mrs. Art Pavin, 338 E. St. Anne St., Rapid City, S. D. 57701

PHEASANT AND VEGETABLE CASSEROLE

Skin the pheasant. Cut it up and put in salt water for 20 min. Drain well, and salt each piece and roll in flour and fry in half lard and half butter. Put in casserole and surround with lots of carrots (whole) and cut up parsnips and little onions. Add to this 2 c. water and bake at 325° until meat and vegetables are tender.

Mrs. Louis J. Peterson, 23 Southeast 80th, Portland, Oregon 97215

PHEASANT HOT DISH

1 4 lb. pheasant, cooked and boned
2 c. soft bread crumbs
1½ c. cooked rice or noodles
1 tsp. salt
½ tsp. paprika
¼ green pepper, chopped (optional)
4 eggs, slightly beaten
½ c. melted butter
3 c. broth and milk mixed

Mix and bake in moderate oven (350°) about 1 hour until firm.

Mrs. Raymond Hieb, Ipswich, S. D. 57451

PHEASANT TETRAZZINI

pheasant
1 tsp. salt
water to almost cover meat

Cut up pheasant and cook until tender. Pour off and save broth. Remove bones and dice pheasant.

3 c. pheasant broth
1½ c. noodles
⅓ c. chopped onion
1 c. chopped celery
1½ tbsp. chopped green pepper
2 tbsp. chopped parsley
salt and pepper
3 c. cooked, diced pheasant
½ can mushrooms
¾ c. canned tomatoes
¾ c. cream of cheddar soup
2 tbsp. butter
½ c. bread crumbs

Cook noodles, onions, celery, green pepper and parsley in pheasant broth. Season with salt and pepper. Place a layer of cooked noodles in greased casserole. Cover with a layer of pheasant, ½ of mushrooms, ½ of tomatoes, and ½ of soup. Add remaining pheasant and mushrooms, tomatoes and soup. Melt butter in separate pan, add bread crumbs and mix well. Place the crumb mixture over top of casserole. Bake at 350°.
Serves 6 to 8.

Note: Sage chicken or wild turkey may also be used for this recipe.

Mrs. Virginia Uresk, 3327 W. Rapid, Rapid City, S. D. 57701

PHEASANT PIE

Cook up 2 cut-up pheasants in water to nearly cover. Add salt and pepper as desired. When almost tender, drain the broth and thicken if you want gravy. Some milk may be used if more gravy is needed. Place pieces of pheasant in bottom of a greased casserole. Add gravy. Top with your favorite baking-powder biscuits. Bake in hot oven until biscuits are brown. (400°)
Serves 6 to 8.

Mrs. Virginia Uresk, 3327 W. Rapid, Rapid City, S. D. 57701

BRAISED PHEASANT WITH MUSHROOMS

1 pheasant, cut in pieces
¼ c. pancake flour
¼ c. butter
1 c. mushrooms
3 tbsp. chopped onion
½ c. stock (or 1 chicken bouillon cube in ½ c. hot water)
1 tbsp. lemon juice
½ tsp. salt
¼ tsp. black pepper

Coat pieces of pheasant with pancake flour. Brown in the butter until golden brown. Remove pheasant from skillet and saute mushrooms and onion in the remaining butter until slightly browned. Return meat to skillet; add the stock, lemon juice and seasonings. Cover and simmer 1 hour or until tender. Remove cover the last 10-15 minutes of cooking to recrisp meat.

Dolores Van Den Hoek, RR #2, Stickney, S. D. 57375

WILD GAME BIRDS

1 pheasant
flour
shortening for browning
1 bay leaf
rind and juice from ¼ lemon
celery leaves or celery salt to taste
1 large onion
⅛ tsp. thyme
1 tsp. Worcestershire sauce
⅛ tsp. tarragon
1 tsp. salt

Split pheasant in half lengthwise or have the breasts skinned out. Soak in cold water 30 min. Brown floured pheasant. Add just enough water to cover birds and then add the above ingredients.

Mrs. Dave Robin, PO Box #463, Upton, Wyoming 82730

PHEASANT SAUTERNE

2-3 pheasants, cut in 4 pieces each
flour
seasoned salt
pepper
1 large onion, chopped
1 c. celery, cut in small pieces
1 c. butter
1 c. white sauterne wine

Flour, salt and pepper lightly. Brown pheasant, onion and celery in the cup of melted butter. When nicely browned add enough water to cover the game well. Now pour your cup of white sauterne wine over this, turn flame down and simmer slowly for 2-3 hours. Add water as necessary and turn as necessary to prevent sticking or burning. Over-cooking is not a problem.
The juice from this is delicious served over bread that has been dried out and lightly browned in a very low oven (175-200°) and wild rice.

Note: This recipe is excellent for very old birds and can also be used for rabbit.

Mrs. Norman R. Hale, 923 Eighth Avenue S. E., Aberdeen, S. D. 57401

PHEASANT HUNTER'S STYLE

2 pheasant
4 tbsp. olive oil
2 to 3 cloves garlic
1 tsp. rosemary, dry or fresh
salt
pepper
⅓ c. wine vinegar or dry sherry

Cut pheasant into sections, wash, drain but do not dry. In an iron skillet, place olive oil and sliced cloves of garlic. Brown garlic slightly. Add sections of pheasant, season with salt, a little pepper and rosemary. Cover skillet and let pheasant cook slowly in its own juice for about one hour or until meat appears tender when tested with a fork. If, while cooking, meat becomes too dry, add about ½ c. water. When meat is cooked, add vinegar or sherry and turn off fire. Cover skillet immediately and let meat steam for about five minutes so vinegar or sherry will permeate meat. When serving, pour cooking juice over pheasant.

The delightful flavor of pheasant is complimented when served with wild rice and a romaine salad.

Mrs. Bootsie Gunkel, 908 River St., Chamberlain, S. D. 57325

PHEASANT SOUP

boney pieces from several pheasants
water to cover pieces well
1 tsp. salt
1 bay leaf
pepper to season lightly
½ c. raw rice
1 c. raw carrots, sliced ½″ pieces
1 very small onion

Clean and wash boney pieces of pheasant well. Put in kettle with enough water to sufficiently cover pieces and add salt and bay leaf. Cook until meat is tender enough to fall from bones. A pressure cooker may be used for this process. Remove meat and bay leaf from broth. Discard bay leaf. Remove meat from bones leaving in as many large pieces as possible. Return meat and add a few grains of pepper. Add uncooked rice and carrots. Cut onion in quarters and add. Simmer mixture for about 1 hr. or until carrots and rice are tender and have taken up most of broth. Serve in soup bowls with crisp crackers as an accompaniment.
Serves 4-6.

Miss Evelyn Peterson, RR #2, Emery, S. D. 57332

PHEASANT CHOP SUEY

4 tbsp. butter or salad oil
2 med. onions, chopped
4 outside stalks celery, chopped
½ lb. fresh mushrooms, sliced through stem
½ c. boiling pheasant stock or bean liquid
½ tsp. salt
½ tsp. pepper
2 c. cooked pheasant
1 can bean sprouts, drained
2 tbsp. cornstarch
1 tsp. sugar
½ c. cold bean sprout liquid
1 tbsp. soy sauce
hot boiled rice

Cook pheasant in salted water till done. Older birds may be used this way. Pick meat from bones.

Heat fat or oil over low heat in a large heavy pan or dutch oven. Add onions, celery and mushrooms, cover and cook over low heat until celery is almost tender, about 10 min. Add ½ c. boiling stock, salt and pepper; simmer 5 min.

Add pheasant cut into matchlike slivers, also drained sprouts. Mix cornstarch with ½ c. cold bean sprout juice and add soy sauce. Add ½ c. of hot pheasant mixture and mix well, then pour all back into remaining pheasant mixture. Cook, stirring constantly, until mixture thickens.

Serve with additional soy sauce over hot boiled rice.

Serves 8 generously and is delicious.

Mrs. William Wage, Groton, S. D. 57445

CHOW MEIN

1 lb. cooked pheasant meat, cut in small chunks
1 c. celery, chopped
1 c. onion, chopped
shortening for frying
1 can bean sprouts
salt and pepper
3 tbsp. La Choy brown gravy
water to cover

Put meat, celery and onions in frying pan wtih a little shortening and brown this nicely. Add the rest of the ingredients and let simmer for about 1 hr. If it gets too thick add more water.

Mrs. Rudy Scholl, RR #1, Box 64, Madison, S. D. 57042

WILD PHEASANT AND DUMPLINGS

2 cut-up pheasants
½ tsp. parsley flakes
½ tsp. salt
½ tsp. pepper
1 bay leaf
4 tbsp. white wine
1 can cream of chicken soup
4 tbsp. butter

Place cut up pheasant in large stewpot with water to cover. Add parsley flakes, salt, pepper, bay leaf and wine. Boil approximately 1½ hrs. or until tender. Remove pieces from broth. Add cream of chicken soup and butter.

Dumplings:

1½ c. Bisquick
dash curry powder
½ c. milk

In mixing bowl combine Bisquick, milk and curry powder. Roll out on floured board. Cut in strips and drop in boiling broth. Cook ten min. uncovered. Cover and cook 10 min. more.
Serves 6.

Mrs. Dorothy Williams, 10032 Deadwood Ave., Ellsworth AFB, S. D. 57706

BARBECUE PHEASANT

1 pheasant
2 medium onions, chopped

Place cut-up pheasant in shallow pan. Sprinkle chopped onions on top of bird. Brown in oven at 450° for 30 minutes. Heat together in sauce pan:

1 c. catsup
¼ c. Worcestershire sauce
2 tbsp. vinegar
1 tsp. salt
1 tsp. chili powder
2 c. water

Pour over pheasant. Bake in 350° oven for 1 hr. or more if larger or older bird.

Mrs. Keith Eilers, 1238 Beach St., Huron, S. D. 57350

PHEASANT COOKED FOR A HUNTER

2 pheasants
¼ lb. butter or oleo
⅔ bottle steak sauce
1 tbsp. liquid smoke
½ pint whipping cream

Cut the pheasant into quarters; age in refrigerator at least 48 hrs. Form a shallow pan of heavy aluminum foil to fit the broiler. In a sauce pan melt butter and heat till very hot. Slowly add steak sauce, stir briskly and blend thoroughly. Slowly add cream and liquid smoke. Mix well and turn down heat. Puncture the quartered birds deeply with a sharp knife point. These punctures will allow basting sauce to penetrate. Lay birds in pan and salt liberally. Slide under the broiler flame. As meat begins to dry, begin basting with pastry brush. Baste at least every 4 min. Turn birds occasionally.

I copied this recipe from a newspaper some years ago and was submitted at that time by Frankie Heidelbauer, Sioux Falls, S. D.

Mrs. Bob Neuhauser, Kirley, S. D. 57546

PHEASANT MULLIGAN WITH DUMPLINGS

2 pheasants, cut into serving portions
2 c. diced carrots
1 c. diced onion
1 c. finely shredded cabbage
2 c. diced potatoes
2 tbsp. fat (bacon drippings)
salt and pepper

Dumplings:

2 c. sifted flour
3 tsp. baking powder
½ tsp. salt
1 egg
¾ c. milk

Cover pheasant pieces with water and cook. During the last 30 min. add carrots, onions, cabbage, potatoes, fat, salt, and pepper. Cook until meat and vegetables are tender.

Make dumplings as follows: Sift flour, baking powder and salt together. Beat egg; add milk and stir into dry ingredients, adding more milk if necessary to form a drop batter. Drop by tablespoons into hot mulligan and cover kettle tightly. Cook for 15 min. without lifting the cover, to keep dumplings tender.

Mrs. Therman W. Patzlaff, West View Farm, Alexandria, S. D. 57311

GRILLED PHEASANT 'N BACON WITH WINE

Quarter the pheasant by splitting the breast section in half and leaving the legs and thighs together. Season to taste with hickory smoke salt.

Wrap the pheasant pieces with thickly sliced bacon and secure with toothpicks.

Cook slowly over a charcoal fire, about 30 min. (or until done.) Avoid flaming from dripping bacon fat by using a water pistol or spray bottle with an adjustable nozzle to knock the flames when they flare up. I prefer the spray bottle.

Baste often with a red wine.

Optional: Place hickory chips on the fire as the pheasant is being grilled.

Bruce McIntire, Pierre, S. D. 57501

PHEASANT MINCEMEAT

1 pheasant, cooked and ground.
Do not use heart, liver or gizzard.
2¼ lbs. chopped apples
1¼ lbs. raisins
1 lb. currants
2 c. sugar
2 oz. can cut citron
grated rind of 2 oranges
¾ tsp. each cinnamon, cloves, allspice and nutmeg
½ tbsp. salt
1 c. grape juice
½ c. stock
2 tbsp. Spry shortening

Cook altogether 1 hr. Can and seal. Makes 6 pts.

Mrs. Myrtle Warren, 211½ North Broadway, Miller, S. D. 57362

PHEASANT HORS D'OEUVRE

4 pheasant breasts
2 eggs, beaten
1 c. crushed herb-seasoned stuffing croutons
oil sufficient for deep frying

Remove skins and bones from whole pheasant breasts. Cut into bite-size pieces. Dip pieces in beaten eggs then in crumbs. Fry in hot oil until lightly browned. Serve hot. If you wish, make several hours ahead and refrigerate. When ready to use reheat in moderate oven 350° for 10 min.
Makes about 4 dozen pieces.

Mrs. Larry Hanneman, Badlands National Monument, Interior, S. D. 57750

PHEASANT SPREAD

Grind left-over cooked pheasant and mix with pickle relish and a little chopped onion. Moisten with mayonnaise and add salt and pepper to taste.

Miss Evelyn Peterson, RR #2, Emery, S. D. 57332

PHEASANT LOAF

2 pheasants
1 pt. stock
2 c. bread crumbs
2 c. milk
2 eggs
1 tsp. salt and pepper

Cook pheasants in water and remove meat from bones. Finely cut up meat and mix together with other ingredients. Bake in loaf pan, one hour at 350°.
Serves 8.

Mrs. Leo Guenther, 1020 South Main St., Redfield, S. D. 57469

PHEASANT BURGERS

1 lb. ground raw pheasant meat
1 egg, beaten slightly
⅔ c. heavy cream
1 small onion, chopped
½ tsp. salt
pepper to taste
½ c. flour

Combine all ingredients to make a blended meat mixture. Form into thin patties; fry in shortening until brown on both sides. (For variation a can of cream of chicken soup or mushroom soup can be added to the patties after they are fried. This makes a good gravy. Cover skillet and simmer about ½ hr.)

Mrs. Henry Walz, Freeman, S. D. 57029

PHEASANT BURGER IN GRAVY

Take pheasant breast and thigh and grind. Mix onion to taste; add salt and pepper. Form patties; fry until lightly brown. Pour milk and cream over patties. Simmer slowly for 20 to 25 min. This makes a nice gravy.

Mrs. Leo Guenthner, 1020 South Main, Redfield, S. D. 57469

PHEASANT BURGER

1 uncooked boned pheasant
½ lb. side pork, cut in cubes
1 tsp. salt
¼ tsp. pepper
½ tsp. sausage seasonings
⅛ tsp. garlic salt

Add seasoning to unground meat, then grind.
Make patties ½ in. thick and about 3 to 4 in. in diameter. Dip in flour and fry both sides.

Mrs. J. J. Rath, Box "F", Leola, S. D. 57456

SNIPE

dressed snipe
1 slice of bread per bird
melted butter
seasoned flour

Place a piece of bread under each bird to catch the drippings. Butter and dredge with flour, salt and pepper. Roast 20-25 minutes or until tender with a sharp fire. When done cut bread in diamond shapes, each piece large enough to stand one bird up on it. Place the rest of the bread slanted in the dish, and cover with enough gravy to moisten the bread. Garnish with slices of lemon.

Karl M. Rottluff, MD, PO Box #1822, Sante Fe, New Mexico 87501

RUFFED GROUSE AND WILD RICE

16 pieces grouse (raw)
2 cans cream of celery soup
2 cans cream of chicken soup
1 can drained mushrooms
2 cans water
1 pkg. dry onion soup mix
1 c. wild rice washed, soaked in hot water
1 c. white rice

Mix all ingredients except grouse in 9″ x 13″ baking pan. Lay grouse pieces on top of mixture. Salt grouse. Bake, covered with foil in 350° oven for 1 hour. Uncover, continue baking about ½ hour or until rice is cooked.
Serves 6.

Mrs. Donald Sanftheil, 6417 - 24th Avenue, Kenosha, Wisc. 53140

FRIED SAGE HENS

Slice breast meat of sage hen thinly. Dust with a mixture of flour, salt and pepper. Fry until done.

Mrs. Larry Honneman, Badlands National Monument, Interior, S. D. 57750

SAGE GROUSE

2 sage grouse
salt and pepper
flour
3 tbsp. cooking oil
1 qt. half-half cream
parsley flakes

Cut grouse into serving pieces and wash and dry with towel. Salt and pepper and dredge with flour. Place in pan containing cooking oil. Over medium heat, brown all sides. Place in baking dish, arranging close together in a single layer. Pour cream over all pieces. Sprinkle generously with parsley flakes. Bake in preheated oven 325° for 2 hrs. Check after 1 hr. to make sure meat is not sticking to bottom of pan.

Mrs. Jerome Renz, 801 Oakland Street, Rapid City, S. D. 57701

PRESSURE COOKED SAGE HENS

If an old bird, cooking in a pressure cooker makes it better. Cut in serving pieces. Split each side of the breast in two or three pieces. Brown the meat lightly in butter. Put in pressure cooker. Add:

3 stalks of celery cut in small pieces
1 tbsp. minced parsley
2 tsp. salt
2 bay leaves
⅛ tsp. garlic powder
2 dashes cayenne pepper
2 c. water

Cook at 10 lb. pressure for 20 to 30 min. Cool for 5 min. before running cold water on pan to cool down pressure. The broth may be thickened and used as gravy over rice with the sage hen meat.
Also the meat can be fried for a few minutes after pressure cooking if you prefer it that way.

Mrs. Larry Honneman, Badlands National Monument, Interior, S. D. 57750

ROASTED SAGE HEN

dressed sage hen
1 large onion, diced
1 clove of garlic, diced
bacon slices

Sprinkle onion and garlic over the birds, but do not stuff them. Lay bacon slices over the top of the birds. This adds moisture and holds the onions and garlic in place. Roast 350° for 2 hrs. Remove bacon, onion and serve. Unless game is cleaned when first shot it will have a very strong sage flavor.

Karl M. Rottluff, MD, PO Box 1822, Sante Fe, New Mexico 87501

SAGE HEN

Split thawed birds in half lengthwise or have the breasts skinned out. Soak in cold water 30 min. Brown floured sage hen. Add just enough water to cover birds and then add the following ingredients:

1 onion, chopped or
equal amount of instant onion
½ tsp. celery salt
1 bay leaf
1 tsp. parsley
1 tbsp. lemon juice
⅛ tsp. each savory, tarragon and thyme
pepper to taste

Bring to boil, reduce heat and simmer covered, 2 to 4 hrs. or until birds are tender.

Mrs. Dave Robin, PO Box #463, Upton, Wyoming 82730

SAGE HEN WITH RICE CREOLE

2 birds, cut in serving pieces
4 tbsp. butter
3 stalks celery, cut in small pieces
1 tbsp. minced parsley
2 tsp. salt
2 bay leaves
⅛ tsp. garlic powder
2 dashes cayenne pepper
4 c. water
2 c. rice
1 pkg. frozen peas and carrots, cooked

Brown grouse lightly in butter. Add all ingredients except rice and peas and carrots. Simmer 4 hrs. or until meat will come easily off the bones. Cut meat into small pieces. Use 4 cups broth to cook rice; bring to boil, reduce heat, cover, then simmer 15 min., or till the broth is absorbed. When rice is nearly done, add bird, and peas and carrots; heat all together for the last 3 to 4 min. of cooking time. Each sage hen should total 3½ lbs.

Mrs. Donald Sanftheil, 6417 - 24th Ave., Kenosha, Wisconsin 53140

SAGE HEN BAKED WITH MUSHROOMS

Soak sage hen pieces in salt water for 8-10 hrs. Dip sage hens in a mixture of:

1 beaten egg
½ c. canned evaporated milk
salt
pepper
garlic

Dredge in flour and brown in butter or margarine. Remove pieces to casserole and to the drippings add:

1 can cream of mushroom soup
1 c. water
1 can (8 oz.) mushrooms
2 tbsp. dried onion flakes or
¼-½ c. raw chopped onion

Pour this over bird pieces. Cover and bake at 325-350° for about 1 hr. or until tender.

The above ingredients will vary according to size of bird.

Mrs. S. R. Hayward, 2720 Gregory Drive S., Billings, Montana 59102

PARTRIDGE IN WINE SAUCE

3 whole partridge breasts
1 onion, thinly sliced
1 tbsp. chopped celery
¼ tsp. dried tarragon
½ c. white wine
4 tbsp. butter
3 tbsp. flour
½ tsp. salt
dash pepper
2 tbsp. butter
1 egg yolk, slightly beaten
3 tbsp. heavy cream

Cut breasts in half along breast bone. Pull off skins. Place breast, onion, celery, tarragon and wine in large saucepan. Add just enough boiling water to cover breasts. Cover; simmer 30 min. or until tender. Remove breasts and keep warm. Strain liquid, boil to reduce to 2 cups. Melt the 4 tbsp. butter; stir in flour, salt and pepper. Gradually add the 2 cups partridge broth. Cook, stirring constantly, until mixture is smooth and thickened; add the 2 tbsp. butter and simmer gently 5 min. stirring occasionally. Combine egg yolk and cream; stir into hot sauce. Serve breasts covered with sauce.
Serves 3.

Mrs. Donald Sanftheil, 6417 - 24th Avenue, Kenosha, Wisconsin 53140

CREAMED PARTRIDGE

2 dressed partridge
¼ lb. salt pork, diced
1 c. thick cream or
1 can evaporated milk

Cut partridge in serving pieces. Dredge with seasoned flour. Cook salt pork until crisp; remove from skillet and cook the birds in the fat. When done remove and put in a pot with the crisp pork. Add cream or evaporated milk to the skillet. Heat and stir; pour this over the birds. Serve with baked potatoes.

Karl M. Rottluff, MD, PO Box 1822, Sante Fe, New Mexico 87501

BARBECUED PARTRIDGE

4 to 5 partridge
1 14 oz. bottle catsup
1 tsp. salt
½ c. onion, chopped
½ c. sweet pickle relish
3 c. brown sugar

Place partridge in casserole or baking dish. Mix together remaining ingredients and pour over birds. Bake in 375° oven 3 hrs., turning occasionally to brown evenly.

Mrs. Donald Sanftheil, 6417 24th Avenue, Kenosha, Wisconsin 53140

SANDHILL CRANE PIE

cleaned crane
1 bunch parsley, minced
1 onion, chopped
3 whole cloves
1 c. cream
buttermilk biscuits

Cut up crane in serving pieces. Poach in water with parsley, onion, and cloves. When done use either the whole pieces or pick the meat from the bones. Strain water in which it has been cooked and make a gravy adding cream. Or discard water and make a rich white sauce. Add sandhill to this sauce. Place in a greased baking dish. Top with buttermilk biscuits and bake until biscuits are golden brown. Serve.

Karl M. Rottluff, MD, PO Box 1822, Sante Fe, New Mexico 87501

BAKED WILD TURKEY

2 small turkeys quartered
4 tbsp. honey
salt
pepper
½ stick butter
½ c. chopped onion
1 c. chicken stock
1 c. white wine
1 tsp. parsley flakes

Quarter turkey; brush with honey. Shake on salt and pepper and place in shallow baking dish. Bake in hot oven (450°) for 30 min. basting often with butter. Mix onion, chicken stock, wine and parsley flakes. Pour over turkey. Reduce heat to 250°. Cover. Continue baking turkey until done. Approximately 1 hr.

Mrs. Dorothy Williams, 10032 Deadwood Ave., Ellsworth AFB, S. D. 57706

WILD GOOSE

1 wild goose
salt and pepper
2 apples, sliced
1 onion, sliced
2 stalks celery, chopped
bacon drippings
4 bacon slices

Rub inside of goose with salt and pepper. Stuff loosely with sliced onion, apple and celery. Brush bacon drippings or margarine lightly over entire body. Place bacon slices over breast. Roast in 325° oven in covered roaster adding 2 cups liquid to roaster or wrap breast in aluminum foil and roast in open pan, adding liquid. Baste frequently. Roast 15 min. per pound or until tender. Remove stuffing and serve.

Miss Evelyn Peterson, R #2, Emery, S. D. 57332

ROASTED WILD GOOSE WITH SAUERKRAUT

1 wild goose, dressed
sauerkraut
butter
salt and pepper

Stuff the goose with sauerkraut and rub a little butter on the outside. Salt and pepper. Bake at 350° until tender. Serve the sauerkraut with the goose. The goose will not taste of the kraut; it only makes it moist and improves the flavor.

Karl M. Rottluff, M.D., PO Box 1822, Sante Fe, New Mexico 87501

SAUCY APPLE GOOSE

1 wild goose, dressed
2 apples, peeled and sliced
1 can applesauce
¾ c. currant jelly
1 tsp. cinnamon
1 tsp. nutmeg
½ c. corn syrup

Place two cooking apples, peeled and sliced in cavity of goose. Bake in 350° oven 20 to 25 minutes per pound. While baking, baste frequently with a sauce made by heating together applesauce, jelly, cinnamon, syrup and nutmeg. Serve the sauce as a gravy separately or over carved bird.
Serves 4.

Mrs. Donald Sanftheil, 6417 - 24th Ave., Kenosha, Wisconsin 53140

WILD GOOSE WITH SOUR CREAM AND MUSHROOMS

5 to 8 lb. goose
garlic salt
paprika
1½ stalks celery, chopped
1 carrot, chopped
1 onion, chopped
fat sufficient for browning
4 tbsp. flour
½ tsp. rosemary
¼ tsp. thyme
1¼ tsp. salt
1 c. thick sour cream
1 can (4 oz.) button mushrooms

Wash and dry goose inside and out. Cut off neck and wing tips. Season inside and out with garlic salt and paprika. Place on rack in shallow pan. Roast uncovered in 325° oven for one hour or until browned and fat has cooked off. Simmer giblets, neck and wing tips in water to cover. Brown chopped celery, carrots and onion in fat until soft and golden. Stir in 2 tbsp. flour, then blend in liquid from giblets (1 c. stock). Season with rosemary, thyme and remaining salt. Stir remaining 2 tbsp. flour into sour cream to keep it from curdling during roasting. Blend into gravy. Remove goose from shallow pan and place in roasting pan. Pour gravy and drained mushrooms over it. Cover and continue roasting another 2 hrs. or until tender.

Mrs. George D. Wallenstein, 622 North Sherman, Sioux Falls, S. D. 57103

ROAST GOOSE

1 wild goose, dressed
½ c. pancake flour
½ c. regular flour
salt, pepper, paprika
fat sufficient for browning
onion, sliced
bacon slices

Cut wild goose in serving pieces, splitting breast. Shake or roll the pieces in the seasoned flour mixture. (I use a paper bag). Brown in hot fat in iron Dutch oven. Arrange the pieces in layers with sliced onion. Put slices of bacon over top and bake covered at 350° for 2½ to 3 hrs. Makes a delicious gravy.

Mrs. August Herke, Howard, S. D. 57349

ROAST WILD GOOSE

1 young goose 6-8 lbs.
juice of 1 lemon
salt and pepper
¼ c. butter
¼ c. chopped onion
1 c. chopped tart apple
1 c. chopped dried apricots
3 c. soft day old bread crumbs
½ tsp. salt
⅛ tsp. pepper
4-6 slices bacon
melted bacon fat

Sprinkle goose inside and out with lemon juice, salt and pepper. Melt butter in saucepan; add onion; cook until tender. Stir in apple, apricots, crumbs, salt and pepper. Spoon cooled stuffing in cavity lightly. Close opening with skewers and string. Cover breast with bacon slices and cheesecloth soaked in melted bacon fat. Place breast side up in roasting pan. Roast in preheated 325° oven 20 to 25 min. per pound or until tender. Baste often with bacon fat and drippings. If age of bird is uncertain, pour 1 c. water in roaster, cover last hour of cooking. Remove cloth, string and skewers.
Serves 6-8.

Miss Evelyn Peterson, R. #2, Emery, S. D. 57332

Mrs. Verne Crouch, 601 St. Cloud, Rapid City, S. D. 57701

Variation:

1 tsp. sage and (or) 1 bay leaf crumbled may be added if desired.
1 c. chopped raw cranberries may be substituted for the dried apricots.

Mrs. Harold Gunn, R. #2, Lemmon, S. D. 57638

WILD GOOSE

1 goose

Clean and pick goose well but do not skin. Lay the giblets to one side to use in the stuffing. Prepare stuffing as follows:

- Goose giblets
- 2½ qts. stale bread (broken up)
- 1 large onion, chopped fine
- 2 Jonathan apples, diced
- salt and pepper
- sage
- garlic
- 2 tbsp. butter
- flour

Boil giblets until tender, remove skin and chop fine. Combine with bread, onions, apples. Mix well and add salt and pepper, sage, garlic and other seasonings if desired. Moisten and stuff goose. Place goose in roasting pan and spread with butter and a little flour. Roast in 350° oven until done. Allow about 15 to 20 min. per pound. Baste often.

Mrs. David Robin, PO Box #463, Upton, Wyoming 82730

ROASTED WILD GOOSE WITH APPLE STUFFING

3½ to 4 lb. goose (whole)

Stuffing:

- 3 apples, cored and diced (no need to peel)
- 1 c. celery, diced
- ½ c. butter or margarine
- 6 slices toasted bread crumbs
- ¼ tsp. nutmeg
- 1 tbsp. sugar
- ½ tsp. salt
- 4 tbsp. honey
- ½ tsp. curry powder

Basting Sauce:

- 2 tbsp. butter or margarine
- 6 tbsp. frozen orange juice undiluted

Wash bird and pat dry; salt inside lightly and prick the skin under the side of the breast to drain off excess fat during cooking. Saute apples and celery in butter about five minutes until they begin to get tender. Add bread crumbs to apple and celery mixture; add nutmeg, sugar, salt and mix well. Stuff bird; close opening by sewing or lacing.

Spread honey on bird; sprinkle with curry powder. Place bird on a rack (to keep bird out of excess fat) in an open pan and bake in 375° oven for 2 hours. Baste often with mixture of melted butter and orange juice. After bird starts to brown place foil over pan and continue baking.

Skeeter Proctor, Oklahoma Dept. of Game and Fish

ROAST GOOSE WITH ORANGE STUFFING

1 goose, dressed

Roast (covered) breast side up about 30 min. per lb. at 325-350°. (Note: Use lower temperatures longer cooking for a tough goose and higher heat and faster for a tender bird). Pour 1½ c. boiling water over goose at the start.

About 1½ hrs. before goose would be done, remove from oven; skim off excess fat, and stuff with the orange stuffing. Extra dressing may be put in around the goose. Remove cover the last 20 min. and turn up oven to 350° to lightly brown.

Orange Stuffing:

4 c. cubed dried bread
2 c. cooked wild rice
3 tbsp. grated orange rind
1 c. diced orange
2 c. diced celery
1 can (4 oz.) mushrooms
½ tbsp. marjoram
½ tbsp. thyme
½ tbsp. poultry seasoning
salt and pepper
½ c. melted butter
2 beaten eggs
½ to 1 c. warm water

Combine the bread cubes, wild rice, orange rind, orange, celery and mushrooms together. Add seasonings. Moisten the mixture with melted butter, beaten eggs and warm water.

Mrs. Rodney Alexander, Box 693 Keystone Route, Rapid City, S. D. 57701

SMOKED GOOSE

meat from goose
⅔ c. salt
1 tbsp. sugar
1 tsp. saltpeter
½ clove garlic, minced or garlic salt

Scrape edible meat from neck, wings and back of the goose and chop very fine. Stuff into neck skin and tie both ends shut. Rub breast, legs and filled neck with salt to season. Combine the salt, sugar, saltpeter and garlic and rub over meat; place in a crock; cover with a clean cloth and weight down with a plate. Set in a cool place for 7 days, turning occasionally. Drain; cover each piece individually with cheese cloth and smoke. Chill and slice thin to serve.

Mrs. Edwin Syrovatka, 119 Trinidad, Naples, Florida 33940

FRUITED STUFFED WILD GOOSE

1 goose—4 to 6 lbs.—may be skinned
salt and pepper
½ c. margarine or butter
1½ c. apples, peeled and diced
½ c. onion, chopped
3½ c. soft bread cubes
½ c. raisins
¾ tsp. salt
⅛ tsp. pepper
¼ tsp. sage
bacon slices

Salt and pepper the cleaned goose inside and out. Melt margarine or butter and saute onions and apples until tender. Add bread crumbs, raisins, salt, pepper and sage. Stuff and cover breasts and legs with bacon slices. Roast uncovered 2 to 2½ hrs. at 350°.

Baste with the following every 15 min.:
1 c. orange juice
2 tbsp. margarine or butter

Basting every 15 min. is important for a moist well-browned bird.

Mrs. Leslie Rice Sr., Box 546, Custer, S. D. 57730

PREPARATION OF DUCKS

Clean well, draw, season with salt and pepper; add a tsp. of vinegar. Place in a cold water brine (about 2 tbsp. of salt to 1 qt. water) and allow to stand in a cold place overnight. Remove from the brine; dry thoroughly inside and out. Placing the bird in the salt water overnight has a tendency to remove blood clots and strong flavors.

Mrs. Edward Ptak, Philip, S. D. 57567

ROASTING DUCK

Preheat oven at 550°. Dry the duck and have it at room temperature. Season the inside with salt, pepper and sage. Rub salt and pepper on the outside. Put the duck on its back on a rack in the oven and leave it alone. Don't even open the door until time expires. A small duck like a teal should cook 12 to 14 minutes. A mallard should cook in 20 to 22 minutes and a canvasback in a couple more minutes. Use a 550° oven all of the time. Take it out of the oven and quarter to eat with your fingers.

ROAST WILD DUCK

1 wild duck or—2 ducks—to make 4 to 6 lbs.
1 tbsp. soy sauce
1 tbsp. sugar
2 tbsp. honey
3 tbsp. dry sherry
1 tsp. salt
½ tsp. monosodium glutamate

Combine soy sauce, sugar, honey and sherry. Rub outside of duck with this mixture and let stand for an hour, turning occasionally or leave in the refrigerator overnight. Rub inside of duck with salt and monosodium glutamate. Place duck in open pan and roast at 300° for half hour. Then cover duck with foil to delay browning. Continue roasting duck for another hour. Remove foil and raise temperature of oven to 400° for 15 minutes.

Mrs. Bill Seney, 1028 W. Clark, Vermillion, S. D. 57069

ROASTED WILD DUCK

dressed duck
salt
pepper
celery salt or poultry seasoning
1 apple chopped
1 onion chopped
1 c. celery chopped
garlic, if desired
bacon strips or salt pork

Season inside of duck and stuff with apple, onion, celery and garlic if desired. Place in roaster and add a little water or consomme. Cover with strips of bacon or salt pork and roast in 350° oven 2 to 3 hours or until done.

Note: If desired soak in salt water several hours before roasting.

Mrs. Louis J. Peterson, 23 S. E. 80th, Portland, Oregon 97215

Mrs. Edward Ptak, Philip, S. D. 57567

Mrs. Everett Simmons, RR #1 Box 408, Sioux Falls, S. D. 57101

Variation:

Prepare bird as above but instead of covering bird with bacon strips during roasting, spread bacon grease over the duck and sprinkle with flour. The ducks are good served with heated sauerkraut to which you have added 2 cloves of finely chopped garlic, 1 tbsp. bacon grease and pepper.

Elsie L. Schulke, PO Box 252, Faith, S. D. 57626

DUCK A'LA ORANGE

dressed duck
1 onion, chopped
1 c. celery, chopped
1½ c. orange juice

Boil duck in water with onion and celery 20 minutes to remove excess grease. Put drained duck in roaster and pour orange juice over it. Bake at 350° for 1½ hrs. Meat is unusually tender and moist.

Mrs. Russell Jacobs, Box 67, Roslyn, S. D. 57261

WILD DUCK WITH SAUERKRAUT

dressed duck
1½ tsp. garlic salt
1 can sauerkraut
bacon strips or salt pork

Drain sauerkraut and sprinkle with garlic salt. Fill the cavity with kraut. Put ducks in roaster and pour the rest of the sauerkraut juice around the ducks. Lay bacon slices over ducks and bake covered in a 350° oven until tender, approximately 1½ or 2 hrs. depending upon the size of the bird. You can also use a lower degree oven for a longer period of time. Serve bacon and sauerkraut as a side dish.

Mrs. Nancy Brady, Mt. Vernon, S. D. 57363

Laurel Dickerson, Box 88, Hartford, S. D. 57033

Variation:

Salt and pepper the inside of ducks and stuff with sauerkraut but omit the garlic salt. Before baking sprinkle the ducks with 1 minced onion and cover with ½ c. pale sherry wine. Bake covered.

Lyle Jensen, 309 North Second Street, Beresford, S. D. 57004

REMINGTON MALLARDS

dressed ducks
1 tbsp. cooking sherry
½ tsp. celery salt
½ tsp. onion salt
½ tsp. celery seed
¼ tsp. curry powder
salt to taste
¼ tsp. pepper
1 small onion, chopped
1 stalk celery, chopped

Place ducks in roasting pan breast up and sprinkle each with 1 tbsp. sherry. Season each with spices and let stand about 1 hr. Add the onion and celery and ¼ to ½ inch of water. Bake at 500 degrees until breast is brown (about 20 min.) Turn and bake until back is brown. Cover and cook 1 hr. at 300 degrees. Total cooking time, about 2 hrs.
If stuffing is desired, use any favorite poultry stuffing recipe.

Mrs. Calvin Andersen, 708 Vine Street, Hudson, Wisconsin 54016

WILDS DUCKS IN ORANGE SAUCE

2 wild ducks

Soak ducks overnight in a dish pan filled with cold water and 3 tbsp. baking soda.

1 med. onion, chopped
2 apples, sliced
1 stalk celery, cut up
salt and pepper
1 can concentrated orange juice
¼ c. pure honey
2 tbsp. butter or margarine
1 tbsp. lemon juice

Drain ducks and place the onion and apple in the cavity. Season with salt and pepper and place in roaster with a little water. Cover and roast at 350° for 1 hour.
Make sauce by combining orange juice, honey, butter and lemon juice in a saucepan and heat. Baste duck with orange sauce until brown and tender. Remove stuffing but do not serve. Serve duck garnished with orange slices.

Mrs. Oliver Carlson, Seneca, S. D. 57780

Mrs. George Vance, Gettysburg, S. D. 57442

Variation:

After roasting duck for 1 hour baste with 1 c. orange juice every 30 min. Meanwhile combine 4 tbsp. Worcestershire sauce, 2 tbsp. brown sugar and 1 tbsp. butter for a glaze and use during the last 30 min. of roasting. Discard stuffing before serving.

Mrs. J. M. Josephsen, RR #4, Arlington, S. D. 57212

WILD ROAST DUCK WITH SAGE DRESSING

1 duck—soak for several hours or overnight in lightly salted water to which a slice of onion has been added
4 c. bread crumbs
1 tsp. sugar
½ c. raisins
1 tsp. sage
2 tbsp. melted butter
1 tbsp. finely minced onion
½ c. chopped celery

Drain and wipe the duck. Mix together the ingredients for dressing and fill the bird with stuffing. Bake at 325° for 2 hrs. or until tender.

Mrs. Rudy Scholl, RR #1 Box 64, Madison, S. D. 57042

WILD DUCK WITH PECAN STUFFING

1 c. diced celery
1 c. diced onions
1 c. seeded raisins
1 c. coarsely chopped pecans
1 qt. fresh bread crumbs
1½ tsp. salt
2 eggs beaten
½ c. scalded milk
2 (2 to 2½ lb.) wild ducks
6 bacon slices
1 c. catsup
½ c. chili sauce
¼ c. Worcestershire sauce

Heat oven to 500°. Combine celery, onions, raisins, pecans, crumbs and salt; add eggs and mix well. Stir in milk. Stuff neck and body with mixture; close openings as you would a chicken. Place 3 slices bacon across breast of each duck. Place ducks on rack in an open, shallow pan. Roast ducks uncovered at 500° for 15 min. Reduce heat to 350° for remaining time. (Allow 40 to 45 min. per lb.) ½ hr. before removing ducks from oven, mix catsup, chili sauce, Worcestershire sauce and pour over ducks. Complete roasting.
To serve, arrange ducks on heated platter. If desired, garnish with watercress or parsley and orange slices topped with jelly.

Sauce:

Use sauce in pan. Skim off fat. Thicken with 1½ tbsp. flour mixed with 3 tbsp. water. Mix till smooth. Add to sauce and simmer till thick. Pass sauce with ducks.

Mrs. Silvis Bolden, 1520 South Second Street, Aberdeen, S. D. 57401

**Mrs. Therman W. Patzlaff, West View Farm,
Alexandria, S. D. 57311**

ROAST DUCK WITH WILD RICE STUFFING

1 4 to 5 lb. tame duck or 3 wild ducks
1 tsp. caraway seeds
2 oz. wild rice
½ c. water
1 qt. day old bread crumbs
¼ c. minced onion
¼ c. minced green pepper
½ c. minced celery
1 tsp. salt
⅛ tsp. pepper
1 tbsp. crushed dried sage

Heat oven to 325°, sprinkle duck cavities with caraway seeds. Wash wild rice; cook until tender in ½ c. water. Save water; combine bread, rice and remaining ingredients using rice water. Stuff the ducks with this mixture. Place ducks breast side up on a rack in a shallow pan; roast 2¾ hrs. to 3 hrs. or until the legs move freely and are tender.
4 to 5 lb. duck will serve 4 people.
3 wild ducks should serve 6.

Mrs. Silvis Bolden, 1520 South Second Street, Aberdeen, S. D. 57401

WILD DUCK AND WILD RICE DINNER FOR TWO

2 ducks

Place two ducks in roasting bags. Season before placing in bag, and place ½ apple in cavity of each. Add 1-1½ c. blackberry wine; seal and cook 2-2½ hrs. breast down. Use a 350° oven.

Wild rice casserole:

¼ to ⅓ c. dry, uncooked wild rice—cook 15-20 min. until soft
1 c. chopped celery
1 c. chopped onion—vary amount depending on preference
4 strips crisp bacon, broken up
1 small green pepper, chopped
1 can mushroom soup

Pour off excess water from rice and mix all ingredients together. Season to your taste and place in oven in a casserole dish. (A deeper dish is better than a wide flat one.) Cook 1-2 hrs. at 350°.

Tom Kuck, Game, Fish & Parks, 614 6th Ave. SW, Aberdeen, S. D. 57401

WILD DUCK WITH ORANGE RICE STUFFING

3 wild ducks (1½ to 2 lb. each)
salt and pepper

Dressing:

1½ c. cooked rice
3 tbsp. melted butter or margarine
2 c. orange sections
1 c. finely chopped celery leaves
⅛ tsp. ground mace
⅛ tsp. ground nutmeg
½ tsp. salt
dash of pepper
1 egg slightly beaten
1 c. diced onion
2 c. diced celery
¼ c. melted butter or margarine
½ c. Red Port wine
½ c. currant jelly

Heat oven to 450°. Wash ducks, pat dry inside and out. Prepare dressing by combining rice, melted butter or margarine, orange sections, celery leaves, mace, nutmeg, salt, dash of pepper and egg in large bowl. Toss gently. Fill ducks loosely with rice stuffing, fasten openings with skewers; lace closed. Sprinkle ducks with salt and pepper. Place diced onion and celery on bottom of shallow roasting pan. Place ducks over vegetables. Brush with melted butter or margarine. Roast 30 to 45 min. Transfer ducks to warm platter. Keep warm. Discard all fat left in pan. Place pan over medium heat; add Port wine. Bring to boiling. Stir in currant jelly. Cook 1 min. Strain sauce into sauceboat. Garnish platter with watercress if desired. Makes 4 to 6 servings.

Mrs. Art Pavin, 338 E. St. Anne, Rapid City, S. D. 57701

WATERFOWL GIBLETS WITH MUSHROOMS AND ONIONS

1 lb. white onions, peeled
1 lb. fresh mushrooms
1 lb. giblets (necks, hearts, gizzards)
¼ c. butter
1 tbsp. lemon juice
salt, pepper

Cook onions in salt water 10 minutes. Drain except for ½ c. liquid. Saute mushrooms and giblets in butter and lemon juice for 15 min. Add onions and simmer until giblets are easily pierced with fork.

Mrs. Donald Sanftheil, 6417 - 24th Ave., Kenosha, Wisconsin 53140

WILD DUCK IN MUSHROOM SAUCE

dressed ducks
flour seasoned with salt, pepper and sage
vegetable oil
sliced onion
1 can mushroom soup
1 c. milk

Prepare birds and cut into serving pieces. Soak overnight in salt water in refrigerator. Dry pieces. Dip in seasoned flour and brown in a skillet with vegetable oil. Place pieces in a small roaster and add sliced onions and a can of mushroom soup mixed with milk. Bake at a low heat until tender.
Note: Cream of chicken soup can be substituted for cream of mushroom soup.
This recipe can also be used for pheasant or grouse.

Mrs. Albinus Dosch, Box 238, Dupree, S. D. 57623

MALLARD SUPREME

dressed duck
seasoned flour (salt and pepper)
¼ lb. margarine
1 large can condensed milk

Cut the duck in small pieces for frying as you do chicken. Roll in seasoned flour. Place the margarine in roaster or heavy pan. Brown the floured pieces on both sides. Pour condensed milk over this and cover. Cook in 375° oven until tender. If it begins to get dry add a small amount of water. Discard the condensed milk mixture and serve only the meat. Very different, rich and tasty.

Mrs. Lyle W. Sanborn, Hurley, S. D. 57036

OVEN-BAKED DUCK

2 ducks (mallard size)
1 can onion soup
shortening

Cut duck into parts as you would do for a chicken. Brown these pieces in a cast-iron skillet with ½ to ¾ inch of melted shortening. When all pieces are well browned, lay the breasts, meat side down, in the skillet and put the other parts around the breasts. Pour onion soup over the browned meat and cover the skillet. Place in 250° oven and bake for 2 hours.
Serves 4.

Mr. Lyle Johnson, Brandon, South Dakota 57005

DUCK AND WILD RICE CASSEROLE

1 duck
½ c. wild rice
1 pkg. dry onion soup mix
¾ c. water
1 small can mushrooms
1 tsp. salt
½ tsp. oregano
¼ tsp. curry powder
2 tbsp. grated orange rind

Cut duck into serving pieces and place in a casserole dish or roasting pan. Add the wild rice between the pieces of duck and cover with onion soup. Add the water and mushrooms. Sprinkle with seasonings and bake covered at 350° for 2 hrs. Add additional water if needed. Serves 4.

Mrs. Robert Jesme, Gary, S. D. 57237

WILD DUCK SUPREME

1 2 to 3 lb. wild duck, cut in 1 to 2-inch pieces
shortening sufficient for browning
1 c. diced celery
1 c. diced green peppers
1 small onion, diced
1 tbsp. Worcestershire sauce
½ c. dark syrup
1 to 1½ c. sauterne or other white wine
1 medium can mushrooms
seasoned salt and pepper to taste

Brown duck in frying pan; remove from pan and place in small roaster or baking dish. Add remaining ingredients to drippings in frying pan; mix well. Thicken if desired. Pour sauce over duck. Bake at 300° to 325° for 2 hours or until tender, basting occasionally. Serve with steamed rice.
Yield 4 to 6 servings.

Florence Blackburn, Bison, S. D. 57620

COOT STEW

1 coot
1 medium onion, chopped
2 tbsp. butter or lard
salt, pepper
caraway seed (optional)
⅛ tsp. ground allspice

Clean coot and remove all fat from meat. Wash well. Put in salt water overnight; drain and rinse well. Fry onion in butter or lard. When golden brown add drained cut up meat and brown well. Season with salt and pepper, caraway seed and pinch of ground allspice. When brown add enough water to almost cover meat. Simmer till well done. Thicken gravy with the following:

⅓ c. flour
½ c. table cream or half and half

Stir thickening into stew and boil about 1 minute. Serve with dumplings or mashed potatoes. Do not overcook the meat.

Helen Proshek, RR #2, Montgomery, Minn. 56069

MARINATED PRAIRIE CHICKEN

2 prairie chickens cut into serving pieces
1 c. dry sherry
½ c. salad oil
2 tbsp. parsley flakes
2½ tsp. salt
2 tsp. paprika
1½ tsp. thyme leaves
1½ tsp. basil leaves
1 tsp. tarragon leaves
½ tsp. powdered garlic
½ tsp. curry powder
⅛ tsp. pepper

Place cut up prairie chicken in a tight container or a plastic bag. Set aside. Combine all ingredients and pour over prairie chicken. Cover tightly. Refrigerate 12 hrs. or longer. Remove from marinade. Place on grill over hot charcoal; broil for about 60 minutes or until tender. Turn and baste often.

or

Place skin side up on rack in roasting pan and bake in preheated oven at 350° for 1 hr., or until tender. Baste frequently with marinade. Serve with corn on the cob or rice and a tossed salad.

Karl M. Rottluff, M.D., PO Box #1822, Sante Fe, New Mexico 87501

SCALLOPED PRAIRIE CHICKEN

1 prairie chicken
2 tsp. vegetable oil
1 tbsp. cornstarch
1 c. milk
1 c. rich cream
1 tsp. salt
¼ tsp. pepper
1 pint fresh breadcrumbs
½ can sliced mushrooms
melted butter
½ c. bread crumbs

Boil chicken whole in salted water until very tender. Cool. Pull off skin. Cut meat, light and dark, into small pieces, making about a pint. Heat vegetable oil in sauce pan; add cornstarch, stirring constantly to prevent burning. Add milk gradually, cook 5 min. Add cream, salt and pepper. Butter a baking dish. Put in a layer of sauce, then a layer of breadcrumbs, then chicken, mushroom, continuing layers until all crumbs and chicken are used. Add remaining sauce last. Cover top with ½ c. breadcrumbs moistened with melted butter. Bake in 400° oven until a rich brown, about 20 min.
Serves 4.

Mrs. Donald Sanftheil, 6417 - 24th Ave., Kenosha, Wisconsin 53140

FRIED PRAIRIE CHICKEN

1 young prairie chicken
salt and pepper
flour
4 tbsp. fat

Clean prairie chicken, dress and cut into serving portions. Plunge into cold water; drain thoroughly but do not wipe dry. Season well with salt and pepper and dredge with flour. Cook chicken slowly in hot fat. When chicken is brown and tender, about 1 hr., remove to a hot platter. Make cream gravy and serve with the prairie chicken.

Mrs. Edwin Syrovatka, 119 Trinidad, Naples, Florida 33940

ROASTED PRAIRIE CHICKEN

1 dressed prairie chicken
celery leaves
½ apple
melted butter or margarine

Wash chicken and pat dry. Stuff cavity with celery leaves and apple. Truss into shape. Roast in 425° oven 30-40 minutes. Baste frequently with melted butter or margarine. Remove stuffing before serving. Serves 2-3.

Mrs. Donald Sanftheil, 6417 - 24th Ave., Kenosha, Wisconsin 53140

Mrs. George D. Wallenstein, 622 North Sherman, Sioux Falls, S. D. 57103

BAKED PRAIRIE CHICKEN

1 prairie chicken
¼ c. flour
½ tsp. salt
¼ tsp. pepper
½ tsp. savory
dash of thyme and basil
1 slice bacon
¼ c. butter

Dredge bird with flour, salt, pepper and savory. Sprinkle thyme and basil on strip of bacon; roll up and fasten with toothpicks. Place bacon roll in body cavity and close the opening. Brown bird in melted butter in skillet. Transfer to baking dish. Cover and bake in 325° oven for 60 minutes or until tender. Make gravy with milk or light cream if desired.

Jane Upchurch, 3910 Yucca Drive, Rapid City, S. D. 57701

PRAIRIE CHICKEN

prairie chicken
salt
pepper
paprika
flour
¼ lb. butter
1 c. stock
1 lemon-juice
1 onion finely diced
4 carrots diced
parsley
2 cloves
3 bay leaves
4 peppercorns, crushed
½ c. claret or burgundy wine

Cut in sections for frying (similar to chicken), wipe dry and season with salt, pepper and paprika. Dredge in flour and brown in butter. When brown, add stock, lemon juice, onion, carrots, several sprigs of parsley, cloves, bay leaves and peppercorns. Cover pan and cook until tender. Add claret or burgundy wine during the last 30 min. of cooking.

Mrs. Edward Ptak, Philip, S. D. 57567

FILLETED GROUSE BREAST IN CASSEROLE

4-5 filleted grouse breasts
flour
shortening for frying
1 can cream of chicken soup
1 tbsp. onion salt
½ c. diced celery
½ c. finely diced carrot
1 can (4 oz.) mushrooms
½ c. melted butter
salt and pepper

With fine sharp knife, remove meat from grouse breasts as one large piece; then cut lengthwise into fillets. Flour and brown in hot fat. Layer brown pieces in 2 layers in casserole with remaining ingredients. Bake 1½ hrs. covered. Remove cover for the last 15 min. (325°).

Note: Remaining grouse can be cooked in pressure cooker, the meat removed from the bones and used in soups, casseroles, etc.

This recipe works well for pheasant, quail, partridge, prairie chicken and sage hen also.

Mrs. Rodney Alexander, Box 693, Keystone Route, Rapid City, S. D. 57701

BAKED GROUSE WITH STUFFING

2 grouse (split in half down the back)
2 c. bread stuffing seasoned with sage
seasoned flour
cooking oil

Pat the bread stuffing in a 9 inch square pan. Roll the grouse in flour which has been seasoned with pepper and salt. Brown in cooking oil. Lay grouse on the stuffing and cover with foil. Bake at 325° for 1 hr. (for young birds). Remove foil and return to oven for 10 minutes to crisp.
Serves 4.

Mrs. C. D. Bartholow, 975 Illinois St. S. W., Huron, S. D. 57350

BRAISED BREAST OF GROUSE

½ c. shortening
2 breasts of grouse
salt and pepper
1½ c. cold water
1 small carrot, sliced
1 small onion, sliced
1 stalk celery
2 sprigs parsley
½ bay leaf
4 tbsp. flour
¾ c. canned tomatoes
1 tsp. lemon juice
1 tsp. minced parsley
½ c. sauted mushrooms

Melt ¼ c. shortening in skillet, add breasts of grouse and saute until brown. Season with salt and pepper. Cover with water; add carrot, onion, celery, parsley and bay leaf. Simmer until tender. Remove grouse and strain stock. Melt remaining fat, add flour and blend. Add stock and tomatoes gradually, stirring constantly. Add lemon juice, parsley, mushrooms, salt and pepper to taste. Reheat grouse in sauce.

Mrs. Edwin Syrovatka, 119 Trinidad, Naples, Florida 33940

WILD GROUSE DELUXE

3 grouse, cleaned and cut in serving pieces
1 egg slightly beaten
½ c. milk
1 tsp. salt
1 tsp. pepper
garlic to taste
1 c. flour
¼ c. butter
½ c. vegetable oil
1 can mushroom soup
1 c. water

Dip pieces of grouse in mixture of egg, milk, salt, pepper, and garlic salt. Roll pieces in flour. Put butter and oil in skillet and heat to frying temperature. Brown pieces well on all sides. Remove from skillet and place in a single layer in a cake pan or shallow baking dish. Add drippings from skillet to mushroom soup and mix well. Spoon over pieces of grouse. Add water to bottom of cake pan. Cover with aluminum foil and bake in 350° oven for 1 hr. or until tender.
Serves 4 to 6.

Mrs. Donald Sanftheil, 6417 - 24th Avenue, Kenosha, Wisconsin 53140

GROUSE SURPRISE

8 whole birds or breasts
(Soak in milk overnight)
salt and pepper to taste
1 c. flour
1 stick butter (¼ lb.)
1 onion, chopped
½ tsp. curry powder
1 can mushroom soup
½ c. white wine

Salt and pepper birds. Roll in flour. Brown in butter to which onion has been added. Place birds and drippings in baking dish. Sprinkle on curry powder. Pour on undiluted mushroom soup and wine. Cover with foil or lid. Bake in 350° oven for 1 hr.
Quail or pheasant may also be used for this recipe.

**Mrs. Dorothy Williams, 10032 Deadwood Ave.,
Ellsworth AFB, S. D. 57706**

GROUSE DELITE

Cut bird into serving pieces—flour and brown in skillet. Put in casserole or small roaster.

Mix together:

1 can cream of mushroom soup
1 can cream of chicken soup
1 can mushrooms, stems and pieces
1 medium onion, diced

Pour mixture over game. Bake at 350° for 1½ hrs. Gravy from this is delicious served on rice or baking powder biscuits.
Quail, prairie chicken or pheasant can also be used for this recipe.

Mrs. Russell Jacobs, Box 67, Roslyn, S. D. 57261

ONE-PAN "GREAT GROUSE"

2 grouse
4 strips bacon
vegetable shortening
seasoned flour
1 can Mandarin oranges

Soak cleaned grouse in salt water for 10-12 hrs. Rinse in cool water and drain excess water.

In frying pan, slowly cook bacon. Add additional vegetable shortening if needed to fry grouse. Flour each piece of grouse and fry until well-browned. Remove from heat and add Mandarin oranges. Cover pan and bake at 325° for 1 hr. or if using an electric fry-pan, cover and cook at 300° for 1 hr. The juice from the small can of oranges may be added if dryness occurs.
Serve with rice or potatoes.

Margaret Thompson, Faith, S. D. 57626

BAKED GROUSE

3 lb. grouse meat
seasoned flour
1 can cream of mushroom soup
½ can of milk

Cut up the grouse as you would chicken. If a nice-sized bird cut the breast in slices (steak like). Soak the meat in salt water for two hours changing the water 4 to 5 times. Dip pieces in flour and brown using any shortening you prefer. Season to taste. Put browned pieces in a baking dish and pour over this a can of mushroom soup diluted with milk. Bake in a 350° oven for 55 min.

Mrs. L. J. Mernaugh, 627 North Jackson, Pierre, S. D. 57501

DOVE "HELENE"

dressed doves
1 bacon strip per bird
chipped beef
1 can mushroom soup
1 c. sour cream

Wrap each dove with a strip of bacon. Place a layer of chipped beef in the bottom of a casserole. Arrange doves on top. Pour mushroom soup and sour cream over the top. Bake 3 hrs. at 350°. This can be used for any number of doves, perhaps as many as 8 or 10.

Mrs. Paul Blair, 1111 1st Ave. W., Mobridge, S. D. 57601

SMOTHERED DOVES

6 to 8 doves
3 tbsp. flour
½ tsp. salt
¼ tsp. pepper
½ c. olive oil
1 or 2 garlic cloves
1 c. California red dinner wine

Dust doves with flour, seasoned with salt and pepper. In a heavy skillet lightly brown doves in heated oil with garlic. When browned, remove garlic and discard. Add wine and enough water to barely cover birds. Simmer about 1½ hrs., or until tender. Thicken pan juices with a little remaining seasoned flour. Serve with rice, green beans, tossed green salad and garlic bread.

Glen W. "Lefty" Bauman, 115 Third St. SE, Huron, S. D. 57350

FRIED DOVES

dressed doves
seasoned flour
olive oil
1 med. onion, sliced

Put enough oilve oil in skillet to cover bottom. Coat doves with seasoned flour and brown in oil. Add an onion to the doves. After doves are browned add some water to pan and braise on low heat. Cooking time depends on age of birds but 30-45 min. should be long enough.

Mrs. Larry Hanneman, Badlands National Monument, Interior, S. D. 57750

ROASTED DOVES

Salt each dove on inside lightly. Stuff with sauerkraut and put bacon strips on top of each bird. Put in oven at 400° for about 30 min. or until done.

Mrs. Larry Hanneman, Badlands National Monument, Interior, S. D. 57750

BROILED SQUAB

6 squabs
salt and pepper
butter
6 slices of toast

Split the birds down the back, flatten breast. Wipe inside and out with damp cloth. Season with salt and pepper and put on a broiler. When nicely browned, pour generous amounts of melted butter over them. Serve on toast.

Mrs. George Wallenstein, 622 North Sherman, Sioux Falls, S. D. 57103

QUAIL WITH GRAPES AND HAZELNUTS

4 quails
salt, pepper, flour
¼ c. butter
½ c. water
½ c. seedless grapes
2 tbsp. chopped hazelnuts
1 tbsp. lemon juice
4 slices buttered toast

Sprinkle quail inside and out with salt, pepper, and flour. Melt butter in skillet, add quail and brown on all sides. Add water, cover and cook over low heat 15 min. or until tender. Add grapes and cook 3 min. longer. Stir in nuts, lemon juice.
Serves 4.

Mrs. Donald Sanftheil, 6417 24th Ave., Kenosha, Wisconsin 53140

BROILED QUAIL

Wash and dry quail. Wrap thin strips of bacon around quail. Broil under hot flame 8 to 10 min. Serve with lemon-butter sauce if desired.

**Mrs. George D. Wallenstein, 622 North Sherman,
Sioux Falls, S. D. 57103**

WILD GAME DRESSING

1 c. raisins
1 c. chopped celery
1 c. chopped onion
1 c. unsalted pecans
4 c. soft bread crumbs
1½ tsp. salt
2 eggs, well beaten
½ c. scalded milk

Put ingredients together and pour milk over mixture. Toss lightly with a fork. Use with your favorite game.

Mrs. George Vance, Gettysburg, S. D. 57442

ONION AND APPLES ACCOMPANIMENT FOR ROAST DUCK OR GOOSE

In a casserole slice peeled apples and onions in layers, ending with onions on top. Add a dash of salt and dot with butter. Bake at 350° for 1½ hours.

Mrs. August Herke, Howard, S. D. 57349

QUAIL DELIGHT

3 or 4 dressed quail
flour
salt and pepper
frying oil

Gravy:

1 can mushroom soup
1 can milk
½ tsp. garlic salt
½ tsp. onion salt
1 small can chopped ripe olives
1 small can chopped pimientos

Take 3 to 4 cleaned and washed quail and cut in half. Flour each piece and salt and pepper to taste. Put in heavy skillet with oil and fry until lightly browned. Remove from skillet; set aside. Remove oil. Make a gravy of mushroom soup, milk, garlic salt, onion salt, olives and pimientos. Put quail back in skillet. Pour gravy over and bake 1 hour with lid on.

Rowena Rachetts, Box 654, Spearfish, S. D. 57783

QUAIL AND VEGETABLES ON TOAST

3 or 4 quail
2 c. sliced carrots
2 c. celery, diced
½ c. onion, diced **or** 1 doz. small onions
or 1 doz. shallots
3 to 4 slices salt pork
¼ to ½ c. butter
1 c. chicken stock **or**
1 can chicken soup
flour
toast

Take 3 or 4 quail, split up the back and spread out as if to broil. Place salt pork at the bottom of a roasting pan. Salt and pepper your quail and spread out properly trussed with the breast side up. Surround all of the quail and partially cover them with the diced vegetables. Melt the butter and continue to brush and baste the quail every ten or fifteen minutes for a half hour. At the end of the half hour add chicken stock or soup and continue to cook and baste. This will take about 1 hr. and 40 min. Have toast ready. Thicken stock with a little flour and pour over quail on toast.

Mrs. Edward Ptak, Philip, S. D. 57567

QUAIL IN WINE

6 quail
salt
black pepper, freshly ground
4 tbsp. butter
1 carrot, diced
1 small onion, chopped
2 tbsp. green pepper, chopped
½ c. mushrooms, chopped
3 slices of blanched orange peel
1 tbsp. flour
1 c. chicken stock
½ c. white wine

Rub six quail with a little salt and pepper. Brown them lightly in melted butter and place in a buttered casserole. To the skillet in which the birds have been browned add carrots, onion, green pepper, mushrooms, and orange peel. Cook vegetables 5 min.; stir in flour and gradually add the chicken stock. While sauce is cooking pour white wine over the quail and place the casserole in a moderate oven (350°) for 10 min. Garnish with watercress and currant jelly.

Mrs. Edward Ptak, Philip, S. D. 57567

ROAST QUAIL

quail
1 grape leaf per quail
salt pork, sliced
butter or margarine
½ c. water
1 tbsp. sherry
¼ c. seedless grapes

Heat oven to 450°. Heat shallow pan in oven. Clean quail; wrap in grape leaves if available. Cover with slices of fat salt pork; tie in place with string. Place quail, breast side up, in heated pan; spread with butter or margarine. Roast uncovered, basting often, 15-20 minutes depending on degree of rareness desired. When quail is done remove from pan; remove leaves; place under broiler a few minutes to brown. Add water to drippings in pan, simmer to loosen all bits that cling to pan. Add sherry and the seedless grapes. Serve with quail.
Allow 1 bird per serving.

**Mrs. Silvis Bolden, 1520 South Second Street,
Aberdeen, S. D. 57401**

PRESSURE COOKED SQUAB

4 or 5 squabs
salt and pepper
dressing (your choice)
1 tbsp. fat
1 tbsp. butter
2 tbsp. water

Season squabs. Prepare any dressing desired and stuff squab. Heat pressure cooker, add fat and butter, sear squabs golden brown on all sides and add water. Place cover on cooker. Allow steam to flow from vent pipe to release all air from cooker. Place indicator weight on vent pipe and cook 10 min. with stem at COOK position. Let stem return to DOWN position. Squabs may be placed under broiler if crispness is desired.

Mrs. Ed Markus, Corsica, S. D. 57328

BAKED PIGEON WITH MUSHROOM SOUP

dressed pigeons
salt and pepper
melted butter
1 can mushroom soup

Split down the back and flatten breast. Wipe with a damp cloth inside and out. Season with salt and pepper. Put in a covered baking dish. Bake one hour, basting with melted butter. When done heat one can mushroom soup and pour over. Bake ½ hour or more and serve.

**Mrs. George Wallenstein, 622 North Sherman,
Sioux Falls, S. D. 57103**

ROASTED QUAIL

Take a roasting pan, butter it liberally and melt the butter. Season the quail with salt and pepper and any other seasonings desired. Place in the pan and cover with melted butter. Lay strips of bacon on each bird. Place in hot oven 475° and bake for about 15 min. Reduce to moderate heat 350° and bake until done. During the baking be sure to baste often with the juices and butter. The quail can be served with gravy made from the juices or in any other way desired.

Mrs. Dave Robin, PO Box 463, Upton, Wyoming 82730

OVEN-FRIED QUAIL

6 quail whole (soak in 2 c. milk 24 hrs. in refrigerator)
¾ c. flour
½ c. instant mashed potatoes
¼ tsp. pepper
½ tsp. salt
2 c. shortening

Mix flour, instant potatoes, salt, pepper.
Roll quail in flour mixture. Brown in deep fat on all sides. Place in foil-lined roasting pan, seal foil and bake in 325° oven for 30 to 45 min. Serve quail on your favorite rice recipe.

Variation:

If you use the new instant rice, the addition of four chicken bouillon cubes and diced red and green sweet peppers produce a good flavor and festive appearance. Pour off all but ¼ c. cooking fat (in skillet where you browned the quail) add 3 tbsp. flour mixture and milk used for soaking quail, and salt and pepper to taste. This gravy is delicious over rice.

Skeeter Proctor, Oklahoma Game and Fish Dept.

QUAIL BAKED IN WINE

½ c. fat
2 small onions, cut fine
2 whole cloves
1 tsp. peppercorns
2 cloves garlic, cut fine
½ bay leaf
6 quail, trussed
2 c. white wine
½ tsp. salt
⅛ tsp. pepper
Few grains cayenne
1 tsp. minced chives
2 c. cream

Melt fat, add onions, cloves, peppercorns, garlic and bay leaf and cook for several min. Add quail and brown on all sides. Add wine, salt, pepper, cayenne and chives and simmer until tender, about 30 min. Remove quail to hot serving dish. Strain sauce, add cream and heat to boiling point. Pour over quail. Allow 1 quail for each serving.

Mrs. Edwin Syrovatka, 119 Trinidad, Naples, Florida 33940

QUAIL, SOUTHERN STYLE

2 quail
2 tbsp. flour
1 tsp. flour
⅛ tsp. pepper
2 tbsp. fat or salad oil
¾ c. light cream or top milk

Clean quail. Split down back or leave whole. Dust with combined flour, salt and pepper. Heat fat in skillet and brown quails. Add cream, cover, cook over low heat 25 min. or until tender. Thicken gravy if desired. Serves 2.

Mrs. Larry Honneman, Badlands National Monument, Interior, S. D. 57750

SOUTHERN-FRIED QUAIL

Dry pick quail, clean and wipe thoroughly, salt and pepper, and dredge with flour. Have a heavy deep-fry skillet ready with close-fitting cover ½ full of hot fat. Cook quail in fat a few minutes over hot fire. Then cover frying pan and reduce heat. Cook slowly until tender, turning quail to other side when golden brown. Serve on hot platter, garnished with thin slices of lemon and sprigs of parsley.

Mrs. Donald Sanftheil, 6417 24th Avenue, Kenosha, Wisconsin 53140

QUAIL PIE

Make a rich biscuit dough, using milk or cream for mixing. Roll thin, spread with butter, fold, and roll again. Line a baking pan with the dough. Split dressed quail down the back, lay them in the pan, sprinkle with salt and pepper, and spread each bird with butter. Add boiling water—about ⅔ c. to each bird. Cover with crust, make some small slits to let out steam, and bake in medium oven until done.

Mrs. Dave Robin, PO Box #463, Upton, Wyoming 82730

Small Game

RACCOON AND BREAD DRESSING

1 raccoon
2 tbsp. salt
1 tbsp. garlic salt
1 bunch carrots, cut in chunks
4 stalks celery, cut in chunks
4 large onions, sliced

Clean raccoon, removing every bit of fat. Boil until tender with salt, garlic salt, carrots, celery and onions. When tender, remove raccoon and cut meat from bones. Place in buttered roaster or casserole and cover with bread dressing.

Bread Dressing:
1 small onion, diced
2 stalks celery, chopped
2 tbsp. powdered sage
1 tbsp. turmeric
4 qts. dry bread, cubed
1 can cream of chicken soup

Mix onion, celery, sage and turmeric with dry bread. Add cream of chicken soup with a little hot water and mix well. If more moisture is needed add it in the form of hot water. Spread this on top of raccoon, cover and bake in 350° oven 20 min. Uncover and bake 10 min. more until dressing is browned on top.

Mrs. Donald Sanftheil, 6417 24th Ave., Kenosha, Wisconsin 53140

PRESSURE-COOKED COON AND DRESSING

Cut coon into small pieces and salt to taste. Cook in the inset pan of the pressure cooker for about an hour at 15 lbs. of pressure. Cook longer if it is an old and tough coon. When coon is tender, arrange pieces in a baking dish and cover with dressing made as follows:

8 to 10 slices dry bread
broth from cooking coon
2 eggs
2 tbsp. sage
½ tsp. ground cloves
1 tbsp. salt

Moisten the dry bread with the juice cooked from the coon and add eggs, sage, ground cloves and salt. Bake in oven at 350° until the dresing is browned. This assures a tender, tasty coon without being too fat and greasy.

Mrs. Dave Robin, PO Box #463, Upton, Wyoming 82730
Mrs. Clara M. Poynter, Box 52, Oelrichs, S. D. 57763

RACCOON PIE

1 raccoon
1 qt. water
1 pt. vinegar
1 tbsp. salt
1 tsp. pepper
1 tbsp. brown sugar
¼ oz. pickling spices
1 onion, diced
4 small potatoes
4 small carrots

Gravy:
2 c. broth
5 tbsp. browned flour
2 tbsp. butter
1 recipe baking powder biscuits

Cut prepared raccoon in serving pieces. Mix water, vinegar, seasonings, sugar and spices together. Put raccoon pieces in this brine about 8 hrs. or more. Drain, put in stewing kettle and cover with water. Cook until meat is tender. Add onion, potatoes and carrots. When all ingredients are tender, remove from broth. Thicken liquid with browned flour and butter and season to taste. Place meat and vegetables in a dish and cover with gravy. Cover the top with your own recipe for baking powder biscuits, with a little extra shortening in dough. Bake in 450° oven until brown, about 12 to 15 min. Serves 8.

Mrs. Donald Sanftheil, 6417 24th Ave., Kenosha, Wisconsin 53140

ROASTED COON WITH SAGE DRESSING

Coon is good only in cold, freezing weather. Skin and be very careful to remove scent glands along either side of back bone, and in the small of the back. Also remove scent gland under each front leg. Remove all visible fat and soak in cold water 3 hrs. or over night. Parboil for one hour in fresh water. Remove, wipe dry and stuff with sage dressing to which an apple or two has been added. Roast at 350° or until tender. Serve with applesauce and quartered sweet potatoes.

Mrs. Edward Ptak, Philip, S. D. 57567

OLD FASHIONED COON AND SWEET POTATOES

Cut the raccoon in small pieces. Add salt water and cook until done. Take out of broth and put in baking dish. Sprinkle with sage and pepper. Parboil 5 medium size sweet potatoes and arrange the potatoes around the raccoon. Pour over 1 c. broth and bake 20 to 25 min. at 350°.

Mrs. Clara M. Poynter, Box 52, Oelrichs, S. D. 57763

Variation:

Before cooking soak the coon in salt and soda water overnight. Take out of water next morning and proceed as directed above.

Mrs. Dave Robin, PO Box #463, Upton, Wyoming 82730

ROASTED RACCOON WITH GRAVY

1 raccoon cleaned
beef suet
3 stalks celery, chopped
1 large onion, chopped
1 tsp. seasoned salt (onion blend)
¼ tsp. pepper
1 c. hot water

Cut prepared raccoon into serving pieces (cut off all fat). Render beef suet in skillet and brown pieces. Place in roaster pan and add celery and onions. Sprinkle with seasoned salt and pepper. Add 1 c. hot water. Roast in 350° oven about 2½ to 3 hours.
Gravy can be made from drippings of stock. Use 2½ c. liquid, 3 tbsp. flour and 2 beef bouillon cubes. Dissolve cubes in a small amount of water.) Simmer until thickens.

Mrs. A. Wesley Evans, 229 Franklin St., Rapid City, S. D. 57701

FRICASSEE OF YOUNG RACCOON

1 or 2 young raccoons, dressed
salt
pepper
flour—for coating pieces
cooking oil
flour—for thickening
1 large onion, sliced

Be sure to remove the nodules under each leg, also all the fat. Cut into pieces of frying size. Salt and pepper. Dredge in flour and saute in heavy skillet. When browned on all sides, stir a heaping tablespoon of flour into a glass of water. Pour into skillet. Add more water to cover meat. Add sliced onion, cover and simmer 1 hr.

Mrs. Jerome Renz, 801 E. Oakland St., Rapid City, S. D. 57701

SWEET-SOUR RACCOON

1 raccoon, skinned and cleaned
1 large onion, chopped
1 tsp. dry mustard
1 tsp. allspice
1 tsp. salt
½ tsp. pepper
¾ c. catsup
4 beef bouillon cubes
4 c. water
5 gingersnaps
¾ c. vinegar
¾ c. brown sugar

Cut prepared raccoon in serving pieces. Parboil and scrape off all other fat. Place pieces in roasting pan. Add onion, sprinkle with mustard, allspice, salt and pepper. In separate pan, heat catsup, bouillon cubes, water, gingersnaps, vinegar and brown sugar. Pour over raccoon pieces and roast covered in 350° oven until done. About 3 hrs.
Serves 8.

Mrs. Donald Sanftheil, 6417 24th Ave., Kenosha, Wisconsin 53140

ROASTED RACCOON

1 raccoon
1 onion
3 carrots
½ tsp. pepper
2 tbsp. salt
1 c. broth

Clean raccoon and remove all fat possible. Parboil raccoon 1 hr. in water to which has been added the salt, pepper, onion and carrots. Remove coon from water and place in roasting pan. Add broth, and roast coon uncovered 2 hrs. or until it is tender. Have oven at 375°.

Mrs. Dave Robin, PO Box #463, Upton, Wyoming 82730

POTTER'S COON RECIPE

Cut up the raccoon as if it were a rabbit, using the legs and the loin portion of the back; discard the rest.

Cut off as much fat as possible. Soak in a pan of salt water for 2 days in the refrigerator, changing water at least twice. (Use ¼ c. of salt to a gallon of water). At this point, after rinsing, the meat may be frozen for future use. If frozen, rinse meat again after thawing. Salt, pepper and flour each of the pieces and brown them in a good cooking oil in a skillet on top of the stove. Then place in a roaster with a rack in the bottom to catch the additional fat which will melt out of the meat (coon is rather fat). Pour 2 to 3 c. water mixed with ¼ c. catsup over the meat. Also sprinkle on a little sage, bay leaves, slices of onion and slices of potatoes. Bake at 375° for 2½ hrs.

Remove from oven, discarding the items placed on top of the meat. Remove all the bones. Make a sauce of water, catsup, tomato paste, salt and pepper. (The amounts may vary according to your individual taste, but mix about 2-3 c. altogether.) Pour the sauce over the boned meat. Upon removal from the oven, serve at once, using the drippings under the rack as either a sauce for the meat, or gravy with mashed potatoes. The meat will be very rich and rather dark in color, resembling roast pork in taste.

Note: This recipe has been found to work very well with similar animals such as porcupine and woodchuck or ground hog.

Mrs. Philip R. Potter, 1607 Cedar St., Sturgis, S. D. 57785

RACCOON

1 raccoon

Clean coon. Soak in salted water overnight or longer.

red pepper paste
salt and pepper
2-3 large onions, sliced

Remove coon from salted water, wipe dry. Cover with a coating of red pepper and water made into a paste. Be sure to place on rack with drip pan to catch the fat. Place in an oven at 350° for 3 hrs. for a medium sized coon.

When tender remove from oven and remove coating of the red pepper. Salt and pepper, cover with sliced onions, placing onion in the cavity. Bake for another hour or until tender. Serve with sweet potatoes and bouillon sauce.

Karl M. Rottluff, MD, PO Box 1822, Sante Fe, New Mexico 87501

BAKED RACCOON AND VEGETABLES

1 young raccoon 6 to 8 lbs. dressed
1½ tsp. salt
¼ tsp. pepper
¼ tsp. garlic salt
1 large onion, sliced
4-5 slices fresh pork
dash of Tabasco sauce
1 can whole tomatoes
½ c. water
4 or 5 carrots
4 or 5 sweet potatoes
4 or 5 white potatoes

Remove scent glands from under legs. Place raccoon in large pan and cover with water. Parboil approximately 20 min. Remove from water and let cool. Remove all excess fat and skin. Cut into serving pieces and place in large roasting pan. Season with salt, pepper and garlic salt. Place onion on and around pieces. Place fresh pork slices across meat, add a dash of Tabasco sauce. Add tomatoes and water, cover and bake in 325° oven for approximately 3 hrs. or until tender. Add vegetables around meat during the last ¾ hr. of baking, recover and bake until done. Add more water as needed. Bacon slices can be used instead of fresh pork.

Note: The amounts and kinds of vegetables can be varied to your own choosing.
Young jackrabbit can be cooked in this same way, only eliminate the parboiling.

June Upchurch, 3910 Yucca Drive, Rapid City, S. D. 57701

BAKED COON WITH SOUTHERN DRESSING

1 small coon or hindquarters and loin of larger coon (2 to 2½ lb. dressed)
3 to 4 c. cold water
1 tbsp. salt
⅓ tsp. black pepper or ½ tsp. dry hot red pepper pod

Clean coon as directed in preceding recipe (Barbecued Coon). Cut whole coon or hindquarters and loin into 4 pieces with kitchen scissors or heavy butcher knife. Put into 3 qt. kettle, add water, salt and pepper. Heat to boiling, then reduce heat to simmering, cover and cook until tender.

Prepare dressing as follows:

6 slices white bread from 1¼ lb. loaf
½ c. finely chopped onion
1 to 1½ tbsp. finely chopped parsley
⅓ c. yellow corn meal
⅛ tsp. pepper
¾ to 1 tsp. poultry seasoning or sage
2 small eggs
1 c. coon broth, from parboiling coon or 1 chicken bouillon cube dissolved in 1 c. water.
1 c. milk

Bread should be 2 to 3 days old, but not stale enough to be dry. Tear into coarse crumbs and drop into mixing bowl. Add rest of ingredients and stir gently until blended. Put dressing into casserole. Lay coon over top and press down into dressing. Pre-heat oven at 400° for 10 min. before baking. Cover and bake until coon is tender, 45 min. to 1 hr. Then uncover and continue baking until coon and dressing are nicely browned or for about 30 min. more. Parboiled pared sweet potatoes or winter squash may be baked with the coon instead of the dressing. A tart vegetable such as sauerkraut, sweet sour red cabbage or pickled beets is a good accompaniment.
4 servings.

Mrs. Chuck Callahan, 1701 Tepee St., Rapid City, S. D. 57701

RACCOON

1 raccoon
2 tbsp. baking soda
bread dressing

Skin, clean and soak overnight in salt water. Remove all fat inside and out. Blanch (place in cold water and boil) for 45 min. Add 2 tbsp. baking soda and continue to cook uncovered for 5 min. Drain and wash in warm water. Put in cold water and bring to a boil. Reduce heat and simmer for 15 min. Preheat oven to 350°. Stuff the raccoon with bread dressing and bake for 45 min. covered. Then uncover and bake for 15 min. longer before serving.

Mr. K. L. Harrod, Box 213, Edgemont, S. D. 57735

SQUIRREL STEW

dressed squirrel
½ c. vinegar
1¼ tsp. mixed spices
1 onion, diced
celery leaves from 3 stalks of celery
¾ tsp. salt
¼ tsp. pepper
2 carrots, diced

Wash dressed squirrel thoroughly and cut into serving pieces. Combine the vinegar, mixed spices, onion, and celery leaves in deep pan; add squirrel and cover with water. Let stand for 3 hours. Drain squirrel, brown in 375° oven. Add salt, pepper and carrots and again cover with water. Continue cooking until tender.

Mrs. George D. Wallenstein, 622 North Sherman, Sioux Falls, S. D. 57103

DEEP FRIED SQUIRREL

dressed squirrel
2 egg yolks
4 tbsp. cracker crumbs
fat for frying

Cut squirrel in four portions. Drop pieces in boiling water and boil 15 min. Remove pieces and dry on towel. Prepare batter of egg yolks and cracker crumbs. Dip meat in batter and deep fry in smoking hot fat. (375° F.)

Hilda Heyne, 1036 E. Ohio, Rapid City, S. D. 57701

FRIED SQUIRREL

dressed squirrel
seasoned flour
bacon fat
1 slice of onion, chopped
garlic salt
lemon pepper
1 apple, cut in wedges
½ c. water

Coat cut up squirrel in seasoned flour. Use only bacon grease as shortening and lightly brown. While browning add chopped onion and watch very closely so it does not burn.
Remove from skillet, sprinkle with garlic salt and lemon pepper. Put in covered casserole dish with apple wedges and water. Bake for 1 hour at 300° or until desired doneness.

Note: Rabbit can also be used for this recipe.

Mrs. Nancy Brady, Mt. Vernon, S. D. 57363

SQUIRREL

3 dressed squirrels
flour
salt and pepper
1 c. water

Quarter the squirrels and roll in flour and pan fry as one would a chicken. Salt and pepper to taste. When brown on both sides add water and simmer on top of stove for 1 hour or until tender. Make your favorite gravy.
Serves 6.

Mrs. Elmer Rauscher, 512 North Madison, Pierre, S. D. 57501

PRESSURE COOKED SQUIRREL

1 squirrel, dressed
salt and pepper
¼ c. fat
1 c. water

Cut squirrel into serving pieces, wash and wipe dry. Season well. Heat pressure cooker and add fat. Sear squirrel in hot fat until golden brown. Gradually add water. Place cover on cooker. Allow steam to flow from vent pipe to release all air from cooker. Place indicator weight on vent pipe. Cook 20 minutes with stem at COOK position. Let stem return to DOWN position. Thicken gravy with 2 tbsp. flour if desired.

Mrs. Ed Markus, Corsica, S. D. 57328

WOODCHUCK IN SAUCE

1 woodchuck
½ c. salt
4 mint leaves
¼ c. oil
1 chopped garlic
salt
black pepper
½ c. vinegar
2 c. tomato sauce
pinch of basil

Remove scent glands from chuck. Soak 8 hours in cold water with salt. Cut in 8 pieces and boil 15 minutes. Rinse and repeat soaking process. Rinse again and boil with mint leaves for 45 minutes. Drain and brown with oil and garlic. Salt and pepper both sides. When browned, add ½ c. vinegar. Cover and let simmer 8 minutes. Remove from pan and put into pot. Add 2 c. tomato sauce and a pinch of basil, and cook over moderate heat 1½ hours.

Mrs. Donald Sanftheil, 6417 - 24th St., Kenosha, Wisconsin 53140

OPOSSUM

'Possum is good only in cold, freezing weather. Never skin a 'possum. In dressing, dip in scalding hot water and pull out the hairs. (Like feathers from a chicken.) Another way to do this is to singe the hairs over a bed of hot coals and then thoroughly wash and scrub off in several waters. Remove scent glands.

Remove excess fat, soak 3 hrs. or over-night in cold, salt-water and parboil until quite tender. Season with salt and plenty of pepper and dredge thoroughly in flour. Place in roaster. Have ready 8 to 10 sweet potatoes which have been boiled and peeled. Slice in 1½ inch rounds and place around the 'possum. Cover entire 'possum and sweet potatoes with strips of salt pork or bacon slices. Add enough water to cover the bottom of the pan and add more when necessary, to keep from getting dry. Roast until brown and tender; remove and make thickened pan gravy.

Serve with green salad and corn bread.

Mrs. Edward Ptak, Philip, S. D. 57567

BEAVER

—Young animals only—

Remove kernels in small of back and under forelegs between rib and shoulder. Hang in cold for several days. Poach in salted water for 1 hr. Braise as for beef until tender.

Mrs. K. L. Harrod, Box 213, Edgemont, S. D. 57735

BEAVER TAIL

Hold over open flame until rough skin blisters. Remove from heat. When cool, peel off skin. Roast over coals or simmer until tender.

K. L. Harrod, Box 213, Edgemont, S. D. 57735

GROUND HOG

When ground hog is dressed be sure to remove the kernel from under the front legs to keep from making it taste. Cut up and salt to taste. Roll in flour, put in hot fat, and fry until brown. Then put in inset pans in pressure cooker with ½ in. water in bottom of cooker. Cook for 70 min. with 15 lbs. of pressure.

Mrs. Dave Robin, PO Box #463, Upton, Wyoming 82730

MARSH RABBIT
(or more commonly called MUSKRAT)

3 muskrats skinned and dressed out, rinse in warm salt water. Lay the muskrats in a baking dish and stuff with the dressing given below:

¼ c. chopped onion
dash of celery
½ c. butter
1 tsp. salt
dash of pepper
1 tsp. poultry seasoning
1 qt. dry bread crumbs
1 c. hot water

Add onions and seasonings to melted butter and saute until onions are tender. Combine with bread crumbs and add the hot water to moisten. Put dressing in muskrats as you would a turkey. Cover baking dish tightly and roast at 325° for 2½ hrs.
If any juice is in the bottom of pan or dish, by all means make gravy for your dressing and spuds.

Mrs. Elmer Rauscher, 512 North Madison, Pierre, S. D. 57501

Very good

BARBECUED RABBIT

1 2-2½ lb. rabbit
1 c. flour
1 tsp. salt
½ c. fat

Barbecue Sauce:

3 tbsp. meat stock or water
3 tbsp. chili sauce
1 tsp. Worcestershire sauce
3 tbsp. catsup
2 tbsp. vinegar
1½ tsp. salt
¼ tsp. pepper, if desired
½ small onion, minced
1 tbsp. brown sugar

Clean rabbit and cut into serving pieces. Dust in seasoned flour and brown in fat. Combine ingredients for barbecue sauce; pour over rabbit and simmer 35-60 minutes or longer.

Mrs. Leonard Reinke, Elkton, S. D. 57026

QUICK HASSENPFEFFER

1 rabbit
salt
pepper
flour
fat for frying
3 tbsp. flour
1 c. water
1 tbsp. vinegar
½ (14 oz.) bottle catsup
2 bay leaves
dash red pepper
1 med onion, sliced

Cut rabbit into pieces. Salt and pepper each piece, dredge with flour, and fry in fat until the meat is crusted a golden brown. Make a gravy by adding flour to the fat in which the rabbit has been fried, then adding water and stirring until smooth and creamy thick. Add vinegar, catsup, bay leaves, red pepper and onion. Place the meat in gravy, cover and simmer until tender.

Mrs. Charles Weinberger, Artesian, S. D. 57314

RABBIT OSWEGO

2 dressed rabbits
salt
pepper
½ lb. salt pork, cubed
1 c. pure olive oil
2 cloves garlic, sliced
½ tsp. oregano
1 bunch celery (tops only)

Cut rabbit into serving pieces, dry, then rub pieces with salt and pepper. Pour oil into Dutch oven or heavy iron skillet with cover. Heat oil over medium flame till hot; add salt pork cubes and garlic. When garlic is browned, remove it, turn flame down low and sprinkle meat with oregano; add celery tops. Cover and let simmer for 45 min. or till rabbit is tender. Stir occasionally but don't pierce the meat. A bit of water may be added if too dry.

Note: Once I tried celery stalks as I couldn't get the leaves. It doesn't work. Now I go to any supermarket and "sweet talk" the vegetable man to save just the celery leaves.

This also works well with squirrels.

Henry Mar, 817 First St., Brookings, S. D. 57006

RABBIT FRICASSEE

1 rabbit (about 3 lbs.)
1½ tsp. monosodium glutamate
1 tsp. salt
½ tsp. pepper
½ tsp. saffron
¼ tsp. oregano
bacon drippings for frying
1 large onion, chopped fine
1 tbsp. vinegar
½ c. water

Cut rabbit in serving pieces. Let stand in vinegar brine for 3 hours. Drain and dry. Sprinkle monosodium glutamate evenly on rabbit pieces. Cover and allow to stand in cool place or refrigerator over night. Mix together salt, pepper, saffron and oregano and rub into meat. Heat 1 inch fat in deep skillet. Fry rabbit slowly until golden brown on all sides. Place onion in bottom of casserole. Arrange rabbit on top of onion; combine vinegar and water; pour over rabbit. Cover tightly and bake 275° about 2 hrs. or until tender.

Mrs. George Wallenstein, 622 North Sherman, Sioux Falls, S. D. 57103

RABBIT PIE

1 rabbit
salt and pepper
flour
2 onions, sliced
2 carrots, diced
2-3 potatoes, diced
flour for thickening stew
rich biscuit dough

Cut rabbit in serving pieces. Soak in equal parts of vinegar and water for 12 to 24 hours. Drain and wipe dry. Sprinkle with salt and pepper and dredge with flour. Sear quickly in frying pan; add water to cover and simmer slowly in covered pot for 1½ hrs. Add onions, carrots, and potatoes. Cook until vegetables are done. Thicken stew with flour. Put in greased baking dish and cover top with rich biscuit dough crust. Return to oven and bake until dough is done. (About 15-20 minutes in a 400° oven.)

Mrs. Myrtle Warren, 216½ North Broadway, Miller, S. D. 57362

RABBIT

Cut rabbit in pieces as for frying and soak in salt water 3 hours or overnight. Drain and wipe dry. Season with salt and pepper. Brown in hot fat. Place in a dutch oven and add remaining ingredients:

- 6 peppercorns
- 4 cloves
- 2 bay leaves
- 1 sliced carrot
- 1 tbsp. lemon juice
- 1 c. water

Simmer 1½ hours or until tender. Thicken gravy, add 1 tsp. Kitchen Bouquet if desired.

Mrs. Edward Ptak, Philip, S. D. 57567

RABBIT STEW

- 2 c. dried lima beans that have been soaked overnight in 1½ qts. cold water
- 1 small rabbit cut in serving pieces
- 2 tsp. salt
- ⅛ tsp. pepper
- 1 tsp. monosodium glutamate
- 1 bay leaf
- 1 med. onion, diced
- 1 bunch carrots, sliced
- 2 large green peppers, chopped
- 2 tbsp. butter

Place rabbit in boiling water with drained beans. About 1½ qts. water or to cover. Add salt, pepper, monosodium glutamate, bay leaf, onion, and carrots. Simmer 1 hour. Add more water if needed. Add peppers during the last 15 minutes with butter. Thicken gravy if desired.

Mrs. George D. Wallenstein, 622 North Sherman, Sioux Falls, S. D. 57103

JACKRABBIT

1 jackrabbit
1 bay leaf
2 medium onions, sliced
2 c. water
salt and pepper
shortening for frying

Pressure cook a jack rabbit with a bay leaf, 1 of the onions, water, salt and pepper for 20 minutes at 10 lb. pressure to tenderize it before frying. Continue by frying the rabbit with the other onion sliced.

Mrs. Larry Hanneman, Badlands National Monument, Interior, S. D. 57750

FRIED RABBIT

Skin the rabbit, then cut it up. Salt each piece and roll in flour. Fry in deep fat for 50 minutes. Also good for squirrel.

Mrs. Louis J. Peterson, 23 S. E. 80th, Portland, Oregon 97215

FRIED RABBIT

dressed rabbit, cut into pieces
1 c. flour
1 tsp. salt
¼ tsp. pepper
2 tbsp. salad oil
1 tbsp. butter
1 chicken bouillon cube
½ c. hot water

Dredge rabbit pieces in seasoned flour until well-coated. Brown on all sides in the salad oil and butter in skillet. Dissolve bouillon in the hot water and pour over the meat. Cover and cook for 45 min. over low heat.

Mrs. L. Ramsdell, 808 6th Ave. W., Lemmon, S. D. 57638

Big Game

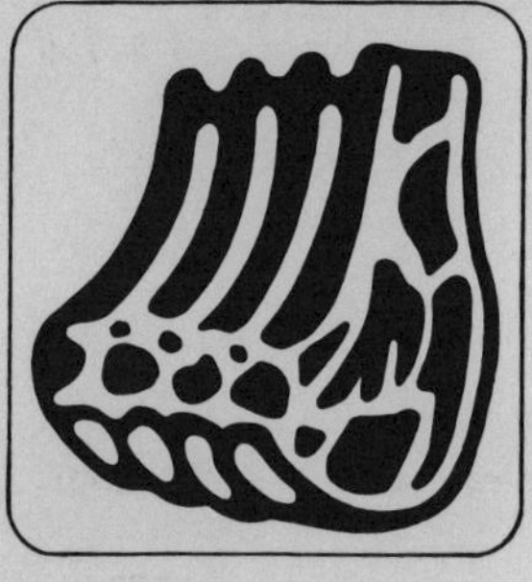

ELK OR VENISON POT ROAST

3 to 4 lb. venison roast
4 c. California Claret Wine
1 medium onion, sliced
1 large bay leaf
½ tsp. dried rosemary
3 to 4 peppercorns, crushed
3 to 4 juniper berries
4 tbsp. olive oil

Place elk or venison roast in a mixture of California Claret, onion, bay leaf, rosemary, crushed peppercorns, and juniper berries. Marinate for 2 hours, turning meat; remove meat and dry. Heat olive oil in Dutch oven; brown meat lightly; cover and bake in slow oven (300°) 30 minutes to the pound. If more baste is needed, use heated wine.

Glen W. "Lefty" Bauman, 115 Third St. SE, Huron, S. D. 57350

CHILI

4 slices salt pork
2 lbs. ground elk, moose, venison or antelope
2 large onions, chopped
3 c. tomato juice
½ tsp. oregano
2 pkgs. French's Chili O Mix
1 tsp. brown sugar
½ c. red wine
½ tsp. black pepper

Chop salt pork and brown in skillet. Add ground meat and chopped onion. Cook 30 min. on med. heat. Put browned meat and onion into large sauce pan. Add tomato juice, oregano, chili mix, brown sugar, wine and black pepper. Simmer 3 hours. (Add water if chili becomes dry.)
Serves 6.

**Mrs. Dorothy Williams, 10032 Deadwood Ave.,
Ellsworth AFB, S. D. 57706**

ANTELOPE DELIGHT

antelope round steak
1 pkg. meat marinade
2 tbsp. vinegar
1 tbsp. water
¼ c. salad oil
flour
oil for frying

Mix ready-made meat marinade with vinegar, water and salad oil. Pour this over antelope round steak and let marinate for 4-5 hours. Lift meat from marinade and roll in flour, brown slightly in frying pan in cooking oil. Mix rest of marinade with 1 cup water and pour over meat. Bake in 325° oven for 1 hour and 45 minutes. The larger amcunt of meat you use, the more marinade you will need.

Mrs. Vernon Martin, 1745 Marshall Road, Aberdeen, S. D. 57401

ELK STROGANOFF

1½ lb. elk round steak
flour
pepper
¼ c. butter or oil
1 c. sliced mushrooms
½ c. chopped onion
1 clove garlic
2 c. beef broth (bouillon cube dissolved in water)
1 c. sour cream

Cut round steak into thin strips (like French fries). Roll in flour and pepper (always salt wild meat after it has been cooked on both sides as the salt draws all the moisture out and leaves it tasteless). Brown in butter or oil. Add mushrooms, onions and garlic. When browned, stir in beef broth. Cover and cook 1 hour until tender. Stir in sour cream. Simmer 5 min. more.
Very good served over hot homemade buttered noodles.

Mrs. Fred E. Welter, 505 Menlo, Sioux Falls, S. D. 57104

ELK MINCEMEAT

4 lb. ground cooked meat
½ lb. suet
6 lb. chopped tart apples
2 lb. seedless raisins
2 lb. currants
2 #2 cans crushed pineapple
3 c. white sugar
3 c. brown sugar
1 c. vinegar
1 qt. meat broth
2 qt. sweet cider
2 tbsp. each of cinnamon, nutmeg, allspice and salt
1 tbsp. cloves
1 tbsp. vanilla

Cook 1½ hrs. Seal in glass jars. Makes 10 qts.

Mrs. Sylvia Higgs, 929½ Kansas City St., Rapid City, S. D. 57701

ANTELOPE BURGER

30 lb. antelope meat
10 lb. fatty beef (beef ribs)

Grind antelope meat and mix with ground beef. Form into patties, about six to a pound. Make them flat. Before frying, season to taste. Serve on split bun with a thin slice of onion, mustard or catsup.
Delicious with a vegetable salad.

Mrs. Roy G. Anderson, Box 101, Irene, S. D. 57037

MARINATED ANTELOPE ROAST

antelope or venison roast or round steak
flavored tenderizer salt
1 can onion soup
salt and pepper

Wash the meat in water with a little vinegar added. (Soak if bloody.) Sprinkle on flavored tenderizer salt. Puncture deeply into roast with a fork to let it penetrate. Tenderizer salt should stand an hour before roasting. Pour over a can of onion soup. Roast until done. Add pepper and more salt to taste.

Mrs. Roy H. Bunning, Faulkton, S. D. 57438

SOUTH DAKOTA SUKIYAKI

antelope roast
1 onion, sliced in rings
parboiled potatoes
large sized mushrooms
tallow

Slice antelope roast while still slightly frozen into narrow strips. Place electric fry pan in middle of serving table. Melt a little tallow in the pan and fry meat and vegetables together.
Everyone cooks and eats at the same time. Season. Dip in soy sauce, mustard or catsup. Eat with boiled rice and an assortment of crackers.

Mrs. Roy G. Anderson, Box 101, Irene, S. D. 57037

AFRICAN PEANUT BUTTER SAUCE AND MEAT

½ lb. antelope meat, cut for stew
oil
1 medium onion, chopped
½ c. chopped green pepper
margarine, sufficient for sauteing
½ c. or more water
salt
½ c. smooth peanut butter
1 tbsp. or more tomato paste
1 tsp. black pepper

Brown the meat in oil. Saute onion and pepper in margarine. Place the beef in this sauted mixture. Add ½ c. or more water. Add salt to taste. Add peanut butter and tomato paste and cook slowly about 45 minutes. (It sticks after the peanut butter is added, be careful). Serve over rice or noodles.

This is a recipe, originally from Africa, which serves very well for buffalo meat, and probably could be used for other meats as well. The African recipe is from a collection of camping and international recipes, and helped finance the troop's trip to the national Girl Scout Center West, at Ten Sleep, Wyoming.

Mrs. Pat O'Leary, Box 641, Belle Fourche, S. D. 57717

MOUNTAIN GOAT CHOPS OR STEAKS

4 to 5 mountain goat chops or goat steaks
(cut into serving pieces)
bacon fat
salt and pepper
1 can cream of mushroom soup
½ can water

Brown both sides of meat in bacon fat. Season with salt and a bit of pepper. Arrange in glass baking dish and cover with the mushroom soup which has been diluted with ½ can of water. Cover tightly with foil and bake for 4 hrs. at 250 to 275°. Very tender and delicious.

Mrs. Ferne Crouch, 601 St. Cloud, Rapid City, S. D. 57701

BUFFALO PEMMICAN

Cut buffalo meat into thin strips and dry thoroughly. Pound the dry meat until pulverized. Mash in dried wild berries or ground up raisins. Hold together with melted suet. Pack firmly in casings.

Proportion:
1 lb. fine meat
½ c. berries or raisins

This is nourishing and keeps without refrigeration.

Hilda Heyne, 1036 E. Ohio, Rapid City, S. D. 57701

CHILI MADE FROM MOUNTAIN GOAT

Use your favorite chili recipe but use ground mountain goat instead of ground beef. Since goat meat requires a longer period of cooking, be sure to let the chili simmer for about two hours and it will be real good.

Mrs. Ferne Crouch, 601 St. Cloud, Rapid City, S. D. 57701

VENISON MINCEMEAT

4 lbs. cooked ground venison
5 lbs. apples (cored and chopped)
½ lb. ground beef suet
4 lbs. seedless raisins
¼ lb. citron (chopped)
2 lbs. crushed pineapple (canned)
2 c. white sugar
2 c. brown sugar
2 tbsp. salt
2 tbsp. cinnamon
1 tbsp. vanilla
1 tsp. nutmeg
3 qts. sweet cider

Cook slowly for 2 hrs. and seal or freeze. Makes 10 qts.

Mrs. Everett Simmons, RR #1 Box 408, Sioux Falls, S. D. 57101

VENISON MINCE PIE

2 lbs. venison meat, well chopped (or ground)
4 lbs. apples, well chopped
4 lbs. all white sugar **or**
(2 lbs. white and 2 lbs. brown sugar)
1 lb. raisins
1 pkg. currants
½ lb. butter (or can use ½ lb. suet
put through grinder)
4 pulverized crackers
1 qt. sour cider, if you use sweet cider
use ½ c. vinegar
4 tsp. nutmeg
4 tsp. cloves
6 tsp. cinnamon
6 tsp. allspice
3 tsp. pepper
4 tsp. salt
4 tsp. mace

Put all together and cook until apples look done and can. Makes about 12 pints.

Mrs. Henry Boeding, Isabel, S. D. 57633

HEART OF VENISON

1 deer heart
5 strips of bacon
1 pt. tomato juice
1 pt. water
1 bay leaf
½ tsp. sweet basil
5 whole cloves
pinch cinnamon

Place tomato juice, water and spices in the bottom of a steamer kettle. In top of steamer place the heart with the bacon strips on top. Cover tightly and steam slowly for 3 hours or until fork inserted in the meat comes out easily. Chill the heart thoroughly, then slice thin and serve cold. Strain the cooking liquid from this and use as a base for venison stew.

VENISON STEW

venison stew meat
2 tbsp. bacon fat
liquid from cooked heart
tomato juice
water
1 bay leaf
4 small whole onions
small whole carrots
potatoes
peas
wax beans

Cut the less choice and less tender cuts of meat and sear in the bottom of a large kettle in which the bacon fat has been melted. After meat has browned, add the liquid from the preceding recipe (Heart of Venison). Add more tomato juice and water in equal amounts until meat is covered. Add bay leaf as this tones down any wild taste the meat may have. Add vegetables and simmer one hour or until meat and vegetables are tender.

Leona Armour, Box 1294, Huron, S. D. 57350

QUICK JERKY

wild game or beef
Mortons (smoke flavored) sugar cure
liquid smoke or A-1 Sauce

Remove all fat from meat—this is important. Cut to any size strips but not over ¼ to ½ inch thick. Rub into each strip the Mortons sugar cure.

Place in oven on rack and set oven between 140°-200°. Leave door ajar so moisture can escape and dry to taste. After the strips are dried you may paint them on each side with a liquid smoke or try an A-1 sauce.

John Heilman, Jr., Miller, S. D. 57362

VENISON LIVER KABOBS

sliced venison liver
salt and pepper
onions
pineapple chunks
green pepper
½ c. melted butter
¼ tsp. garlic salt

Cut ½ inch thick slices of venison liver into 1½ inch squares. Sprinkle with salt and pepper. String on skewer alternately with onions, pineapple chunks and 1½ inch squares of green pepper. Broil 3 to 5 inches from heat for 5 minutes per side. Do not overcook. Brush often with a mixture of the melted butter and garlic salt.

Mrs. Wayne Hook, RR #3, Huron, S. D. 57350

Variation:
Bacon can be added to the skewer of liver and vegetables.

Mrs. Al Ackerman, North Oxford Road, Aberdeen, S. D. 57401

CANNED VENISON

Roast meat, cooking slowly in moderate oven about 15 min. for each pound of venison. Slice-pack in clean Kerr jars to within 1 inch of top. Add 1 tsp. salt to each qt. jar if desired. Add 3 or 4 tbsp. broth. Onion may be added if desired. Put on cap, screwing band firmly tight. Process in pressure cooker 60 minutes at 15 lbs.

Mrs. George Falor, 424 South Lyndale, Sioux Falls, S. D. 57104

JERKY FROM VENISON

Cut slices of meat 1¼ inches thick (preferably from the hind-quarter).

Freeze slightly for ease of slicing. If you like wide thin strips, cut meat in slices less than ¼ inch in thickness. If you wish a thicker jerky cut the 1½ inch slice in three ½ inch slices and cut these in strips ½ inch wide. Do not cut too small as there is some shrinkage.

Soak meat strips in a solution of:

1 c. salt
1 qt. warm water
2-3 c. liquid smoke

Soak for only 10 minutes, no longer. Drain well. Put directly on oven grills, don't overlap. One thickness only. Sprinkle with pepper to taste. Turn oven to lowest setting and bake 3 hours. Turn oven off and let cool in oven.

Mrs. Charles Weinberger, Artesian, S. D. 57314

WILD LIVER RECIPE

deer liver
French dressing
1 tbsp. vinegar
flour
bacon fat
1 medium onion, sliced
salt and pepper
1½ c. water

Take deer liver and slice diagonally into very thin strips. Put to soak overnight in a bowl of French dressing to which a tbsp. of vinegar has been added.

In the morning take each piece out separately, retaining as much dressing as possible, and coat in flour. Melt bacon grease in heavy skillet and add some onion rings. Fry easily until limp, then add liver strips and brown on both sides. Season with salt and pepper. Cook for about 20 minutes on slow heat, then add water and mix thoroughly with flour and grease. Resalt to taste. Cover and simmer until tender, about 1 hour.

Mrs. Fred E. Welter, 505 Menlo, Sioux Falls, S. D. 57104

VENISON SAUSAGE

5 lbs. lean venison
2 lbs. fat salt pork
5 tbsp. sage
4 tsp. salt
2 tsp. cayenne pepper
1 onion
juice of 1 lemon

Grind all meat fine, mix all ingredients. Put into casings or fry as country sausage.

Mrs. Rudy Scholl, RR #1, Box 64, Madison, S. D. 57042

VENISON JERKY

Cut 1½-2 lbs. venison in strips (with the grain) 6″ long, 1½″ wide and ½″ thick. Set aside. Mix together the following:

1 pkg. instant meat marinade
1¾ c. cold water
½ tsp. liquid smoke
¼ tsp. garlic powder
¼ tsp. onion powder
¼ tsp. black pepper
½ tsp. Tabasco sauce

Place meat in container and cover with marinade, piercing meat slices deeply with fork. Marinate overnight in a covered container in refrigerator. Remove meat strips, drain slightly and place on rack, making sure strips do not overlap. Place rack over a cookie sheet in a 150-175° oven and bake for 3-3½ hrs. Remove from oven, cool and store in a covered container in refrigerator. Since this jerky does not have a preservative like the commercial product of its kind, it is necessary to keep it under refrigeration.

Elsie Bak, White River, S. D. 57579

VENISON SAUSAGE

Be sure the fat, ligaments and tissues are all trimmed from the venison.

Use ⅔ ground venison and ⅓ ground smoked bacon ends.

For 10 pounds of the above meat mixture, use the following seasoning:

4 oz. salt
1 oz. pepper
½ oz. sage
½ oz. ginger

Mix all thoroughly. Make into patties for frying, or into rolls, for use. This freezes nicely.

Mrs. Ferne L. Crouch, 601 St. Cloud, Rapid City, S. D. 57701

VENISON CASSEROLE

½ pkg. egg noodles
1 lb. ground venison
½ lb. pork sausage
1 tbsp. green pepper, chopped
1 med. onion, chopped
fat
1 can tomato soup
1 can niblets corn
1 can mushrooms
1 can tomato sauce
salt and pepper to taste
¼ tsp. garlic powder (nct garlic salt)
pinch oregano

Boil noodles until tender in salted water and drain. Saute crumbled meat, green pepper and onion in small amount of fat. Add other ingredients. Put noodles in greased casserole dish and then pour other mixture into noodles. Bake for about 30 min. in 275° oven.

Mrs. George Falor, 424 South Lyndale, Sioux Falls, S. D. 57104

VENISON SUMMER SAUSAGE

Grind together:

4 lb. pork
12 lb. venison—choice meat without cords.

Add:

3 heaping tbsp. tenderquick
½ c. smoke salt
3 tsp. pepper
1 tsp. liquid smoke
3 tbsp. whole mustard seed

Mix thoroughly. Let stand in cool place overnight. Cover to avoid drying on top.

Use sausage stuffer to stuff in casings. Tie shut and let stand in cool place, overnight. (Don't freeze). Smoke for about 4 hrs. Let smoke draw in overnight. Smoke again for about 4 hrs. or to taste. Smoke will draw in. Stand again for a day. Store in freezer. (IF, you can keep it from being eaten.)

Mrs. Roy H. Bunning, Faulkton, S. D. 57438

VENISON BURGER

Remove all tissue and fat from venison.
Take half venison and half pork (fresh shoulder meat) and grind together.
Package for freezing and later use with your favorite recipes.

Mrs. Rose Paulsen, RR #1, Miller, S. D. 57362

VENISON MEAT LOAF

1 lb. ground venison
⅓ lb. ground pork
1 egg
½ c. milk
1½ tsp. salt
1 tbsp. chopped onion
1 c. bread crumbs

After mixing the meats thoroughly add other ingredients and combine well. Place in greased pan and bake for one hour in medium oven (350°).

Mrs. Rudy Scholl, RR #1 Box 64, Madison, S. D. 57042

VENISON NOODLE SKILLET

1 lb. ground venison
3 tbsp. shortening
½ c. diced onion
½ c. diced green pepper
1 c. diced celery
1 (1 lb.) can red kidney beans
2 c. broad noodles, **uncooked**
1 qt. tomatoes
1 (4 oz.) can mushrooms
2 tsp. seasoned salt
1 tsp. chili powder
⅛ tsp. pepper

In large skillet brown meat in shortening; saute onion, green pepper and celery until transparent. Add remaining ingredients; mix well. Cover tightly; bring to boil. Reduce heat; simmer 20 minutes. Serves 8.
Note: This dish improves its flavor when made ahead and re-heated.

Mrs. Al Ackerman, North Oxford Road, Aberdeen, S. D. 57401

Mrs. Wayne Hook, RR #3, Huron, S. D. 57350

VENISON PATTIES

2 tbsp. butter
¼ tsp. onion salt
¾ lb. ground venison
1 slice bacon, ground or cut fine
½ c. cracker crumbs, rolled fine
¼ c. milk
1 egg
1 tbsp. flour
2 tsp. lemon juice
dash of garlic powder
pepper

Combine all ingredients and mix well. Shape into patties and broil or fry until browned on both sides.

Mrs. Herman Paulsen, Flandreau, S. D. 57028

Variation:

Omit bacon and onion salt. Cook 2 tbsp. chopped onion, 2 tbsp. chopped celery leaves and 1 tsp. parsley flakes in butter and add to the above ingredients.

Mrs. Marvin A. Olson, Box 656, Wagner, S. D. 57380

VENISON LOAF

2 tbsp. butter
2 tbsp. chopped onion
1 tsp. parsley flakes
4 crackers, crushed fine
¼ c. milk
¾ tsp. salt
pepper
1 tbsp. flour
½ tsp. oregano
garlic powder
celery salt
1 egg
¾ lb. ground venison

Saute onion and parsley flakes in butter. Add crackers, milk and seasonings. Mix in eggs and ground venison. Mix well and put in a loaf pan. Bake as for hamburger meat loaf.

Mrs. L. G. Vanderbush, Clear Lake S. D. 57226

VENISON APPLE PATTIES

1 lb. ground venison
1 c. cooked long grain rice
1 slightly beaten egg
¼ tsp. garlic salt
¼ tsp. lemon pepper
1 tsp. Worcestershire sauce
½ c. water
½ of a jar of spiced apple rings (5 rings)
¼ c. corn syrup
1 tbsp. lemon juice
2 tsp. corn starch
2 tsp. cold water

Combine first six ingredients and water. Shape into five thick patties and place in baking pan. Drain five apple rings and reserve ½ c. syrup from the rings. Press ring lightly onto each patty. Bake uncovered at 350° for 35 min. The apple syrup and corn syrup and lemon juice should be combined in saucepan. Into the cornstarch stir 2 tsp. water and then add to syrup mixture. Cook and stir until bubbly; spoon onto meat. Bake five more minutes.
Serves five.

Mrs. Nancy Brady, Mt. Vernon, S. D. 57363

VENISON SPAGHETTI

Using your favorite spaghetti recipe substitute venison hamburger for beef hamburger. Add ½ lb. pork sausage to the ground venison (1 lb.). Use extra garlic salt in the recipe.

Mrs. Nancy Brady, Mt. Vernon, S. D. 57363

BROILED VENISONBURGERS

1 lb. ground venison
¼ tsp. garlic salt
¼ tsp onion salt
¼ tsp. lemon pepper
other seasonings if desired for taste

Shape patties, ¾ inch thick and roll in flour. Broil 3 inches from heat for 6 min., turn; broil four min. longer.
NOTE: Handle meat gently when shaping into patties. Too much handling gives the venison burgers a compact texture. Do not overcook as they will be very juicy. When broiling, gently turn the meat only once.

Mrs. Nancy Brady, Mt. Vernon, S. D. 57363

VENISON MEATBALLS IN SAUCE

2 c. grated raw potatoes
1½ lb. ground venison
⅔ c. chopped onion
1½ tsp. salt
⅛ tsp. pepper
¼ c. milk
1 egg
¼ c. butter
3 c. water
2 to 3 tbsp. flour
2 c. dairy sour cream
1 tsp. dill seeds
1 (10 oz.) pkg. frozen peas, cooked

Combine first seven ingredients. Shape into 1½" balls and brown slowly in butter in large skillet. Add ½ c. water. Cover and simmer slowly until done, about 20 min. Remove meatballs.
Stir in flour, then remaining water. Simmer to thicken. Reduce heat; stir in cream and dill; add meatballs and peas. Heat but do not boil. Makes 8 servings.
This is almost like a good Swedish meatball. The dill flavor comes through only as a fresh green pea taste. The onion and potatoes absorb the wild taste.

Mrs. Wayne Hook, RR #3, Huron, S. D. 57350
Mrs. Al Ackerman, North Oxford Road, Aberdeen, S. D. 57401

GROUND VENISON-LIQUID FLAVORING COMBINATION

1 lb. ground venison
1 tsp. salt
1 tsp. Accent
dash pepper

Combine and add to the above:
⅓ c. milk and ⅛ tsp. garlic powder
or
¼ c. sour cream and 1 tsp. onion tops, chopped
or
⅓ c. tomato sauce
or
1 tbsp. lemon juice, ¼ c. water and 1 tbsp. onion, chopped
or
⅓ c. water and ½ tsp. oregano

Mrs. Marvin A. Olson, Wagner, S. D. 57380

VENISON ROAST

4-5 lb. venison roast (oven ready)
1 large or 2 small cloves garlic
1 tbsp. curry powder (Javin brand)

Cut garlic lengthwise in 2 or 3 pieces; slit the roast in various places and insert garlic into meat. Rub curry powder all over the roast. If Javin brand is not available I have found the Red Owl brand is about as good. Place the meat on heavy duty foil, sprinkle a bit of salt on the meat and wrap almost as for freezing. Roast in a 325-350° oven for 3 hrs. Remove meat to a warm platter and make gravy from juices in the foil. Add some beef base or bouillon cubes and some water, thicken as usual and serve. Good with noodles, wild rice, white rice or potatoes. If salt is wanted for the meat try soy sauce instead. Kikkoman brand is best. Cooked this way the roast comes out moist and nicely browned on top with a mild mid-east or Indian flavor.

Henry Mar, 817 First St., Brookings, S. D. 57006

VENISON ROAST

Soak the venison overnight in a vinegar water; in morning drain this off and wash it in clear water. Then sprinkle with salt and add 1 c. water in the roaster and roast this at 350° till tender. (Takes away strong taste and the dark color.)

Mrs. Louis J. Peterson, 23 S. E. 80th, Portland, Oregon 97215

VENISON ROAST

1-4 lb. venison roast

Marinade:
1 onion, diced
1 clove garlic, diced
2 c. sherry cooking wine
¼ tsp. pepper
¼ tsp. thyme
1 pkg. onion soup mix
red and green sweet pepper slices

Place meat in glass or earthenware bowl. Add marinade ingredients. Let stand in refrigerator 24 hrs. Turn meat several times in marinade. Remove meat. Dry. Saute roast in shallow, hot fat until brown on all sides. Place in foil-lined roasting pan, add pkg. onion soup mix and pepper slices. Seal foil and bake in 300° oven for 2 to 2½ hrs. or until tender.

Skeeter Proctor, Oklahoma Game, Fish Dept.

SPIT ROASTED VENISON

rolled venison roast
bacon strips

Sauce:

½ c. pineapple juice
3 tbsp. brown sugar
2 tsp. mustard

Lay bacon strips over the rolled roast covering all sides. Wrap in aluminum foil and place on spit. After the roast is to almost desired doneness, remove aluminum foil and baste with a mixture of pineapple juice, brown sugar, and mustard. Rotisserate for 7 min. until glossy and brown.

Mrs. Nancy Brady, Mt. Vernon, S. D. 57363

VENISON HERB ROAST

3-4 lb. rump, loin or rib roast
1 tbsp. vegetable oil
½ tsp. salt
¼ tsp. pepper
¼ c. flour
2 tsp. marjoram
1 tsp. dried thyme
2 tsp. dried rosemary
1 clove garlic, crushed
1 c. apple juice
1 c. water

Dry meat well; cut several slits in meat about ½" deep. Rub roast with oil, sprinkle with salt and pepper. Combine next 5 ingredients; pat mixture on roast, and stuff into slits. Insert meat thermometer. Pour apple juice and water into a shallow pan. Set roast in liquid—no rack—bake uncovered, in a slow oven 325° about 1 hr. until flour mixture adheres to meat; baste often with liquid in pan. Finish baking about 1 hr. or 25-30 min. per pound (total time), keep basting. Meat thermometer should read 160°-medium; 170° well done. About 6 servings.

Mrs. Al Ackerman, North Oxford Road, Aberdeen, S. D. 57401
Mrs. Wayne Hook, RR #3, Huron, S. D. 57350

VENISON POT ROAST

4 lb. venison roast
flour
1 tsp. salt
½ tsp. pepper
1½ c. tomato juice or water
6 carrots
6 onions
½ c. celery chunks

Dredge meat with flour, salt and pepper and brown in hot fat. Add water or tomato juice and cook over low heat 2-3 hrs., adding more liquid if needed. When meat is tender add vegetables and cook until done. Mix liquid in pan into gravy and serve over ingredients.

Miss Evelyn Peterson, RR #2, Emery, S. D. 57332

BARBECUED VENISON ROAST

4 lb. deer roast
¼ c. vinegar
2 tbsp. brown sugar
salt
pepper
flour

Barbecue Sauce:

½ c. catsup
1 c. water
2 tbsp. Worcestershire sauce
½ c. margarine
¼ grated onion

Dip roast in vinegar and sugar mixture, then salt, pepper and dredge with flour. Place in roaster pan, pouring a little water in roasting pan. Roast in 350° oven. After the meat is slightly browned, spoon the sauce over the roast until done. 1½ to 2 hrs.

Second method:
Put sauce in with the roast right away in a roasting bag. Roast at 300° about 1½ hrs. Stays very moist.

Mrs. Marvin A. Olson, Box 656, Wagner, S. D. 57380

MARINATED VENISON STEAK

steaks—½" thick
clove garlic

Marinade:

1 pt. claret wine
1 pt. water
8 black pepper corns
1 bay leaf
1 tbsp. pickling spice
1 med. sized onion

Rub steak with a clove of garlic and then immerse in marinade for six hours. After marinating, fry quickly on smoking hot grill and serve while hot on a hot iron-stone platter. Dot the venison with butter and garnish with parsley.

Leona Armour, Box 1294, Huron, S. D. 57350

LEG OF VENISON

4-5 lb. venison—remove bones
salt
pepper
crushed juniper berries or allspice
melted butter or fat from smoked bacon
water
1½ c. sour cream or buttermilk

Sauce:

sour cream or buttermilk
salt
pepper
flour

Season venison and rub with crushed juniper berries or allspice, baste with melted butter or fat from strips of smoked bacon. Place venison in prepared pan in oven. When top of leg is brown, turn. Add water when the drippings turn brown. After 45 min. pour sour cream or buttermilk over slowly. Roast until meat is tender. Remove drippings into a pan adding additional sour cream or buttermilk. Bring to a boil and thicken with flour and season to taste.

Kathy Armour, Box 713, South Sioux City, Nebr. 68776

BREADED VENISON CHOPS WITH BROWN SAUCE

3 shoulder chops
½ tsp. salt
dash pepper
1 beaten egg
1 c. fine bread crumbs
fat for sauteing

Simmer chops in small amount of water about 15 min. Drain and season with salt and pepper. Dip chops in beaten egg and coat with bread crumbs. Brown both sides in hot fat. Serve with brown sauce.

Brown Sauce:

2 tbsp. butter
1 slice onion
2 tbsp. flour
1 c. meat stock or 1 bouillon cube dissolved in 1 c. water
1 tsp. Worcestershire sauce
½ tsp. salt
½ tsp. paprika

Brown onion lightly in butter. Stir in flour and brown. Add meat stock slowly, stirring constantly, and cook until sauce is thick and smooth. Add Worcestershire sauce, paprika and salt. Serve over the breaded chops.

Mrs. Marvin A. Olson, Box 656, Wagner, S. D. 57380

VENISON CUTLETS

venison cutlets
flour
salt
pepper
butter or margarine
½ c. or less sour cream
Worcestershire sauce
celery salt (or savory salt)

Trim cutlets, roll in flour, salt and pepper. Brown in butter or margarine over medium heat. Spoon sour cream over the browned cutlets, season with rest of ingredients. Cover and cook over low heat until tender—about 1 hr.

Mrs. L. G. Vanderbush, Clear Lake, S. D. 57226

BARBECUED VENISON SPARE RIBS

3 to 4 lb. spareribs
1 large onion, sliced
Sauce:
1 c. catsup
½ c. Worcestershire sauce
1 tsp. chili powder
1 tsp. salt
1½ c. water

Brown ribs in frying pan, before placing in shallow roasting pan. While browning ribs, combine the sauce ingredients; and bring to a boil. Pour sauce over ribs, then top each piece of rib with a slice of onion.
Bake till well done, about 1½ hrs. at 375°.
Serves 4.

Mrs. Ronald Cordell, 1020½ 4th St. NW, Watertown, S. D. 57201

30 MINUTE VENISON STEAK

6 venison steaks
⅓ c. flour
1½ tsp. salt
¼ tsp. marjoram
3 tbsp. butter
1 small onion, peeled and diced
4 med. carrots, scraped and diced
½ c. celery, diced
1 small can mushrooms (4 oz. size)
1½ c. chicken or beef broth

Mix flour with seasoning; rub well into steaks. Heat skillet, add butter then brown steaks. Place steaks in pressure pan and cover with other ingredients and broth. Put on pressure lid, setting temperature at 10. Cook for 25 minutes. Then cool pressure pan for 5 minutes before placing it under faucet, running cold water over lid. When pressure is down remove lid. Serve. If you prefer gravy, add 1 can mushroom soup after removing steaks and heat to boiling stir to prevent sticking.

Mrs. Harold Gunn, R #2, Lemmon, S. D. 57638

HUNTER'S STEW

2 lbs. venison
2 tbsp. beef suet
salt and pepper
6 carrots
3 stalks celery
3 med. onions
2 potatoes
1 large can tomatoes

Cut meat in chunks; brown in suet. Season and cover with water. Cook until meat is tender. Add vegetables and simmer until they are done.

Mrs. C. D. Bartholow, 975 Illinois St. SW, Huron, S. D. 57350

VENISON STROGANOFF

1 lb. venison steak cut in long thin strips
3 tbsp. flour
salt and pepper
fat
1 onion, chopped
1 c. tomato juice
1½ c. water
1 tsp. sugar
1 can mushrooms
½ c. sour cream

Dredge meat with flour. Add salt and pepper. Brown lightly in fat with the onion. Add tomato juice, water and sugar. Simmer until tender. Ten minutes before serving add mushrooms and sour cream. Serves 4.

Mrs. Leonard Reinke, Box 267, Elkton, S. D. 57026

VENISON BACKSTRAP BARBECUE

This cut lies along both sides of backbone; it is equivalent to the rib eye in beef and may extend into loin.
Strip out backstrap in one piece removing bones if animal is large. Put on long skewer or lay on rack over broiler pan. Wraps strips of bacon around meat.
Broil about 5 minutes per side for backstrap 2 inches thick. Brush often with your favorite barbecue sauce. (Reduce sugar one fourth). Or, you can use a mixture of ½ c. melted butter and ¼ tsp. garlic salt.

Mrs. Wayne Hook, RR #3, Huron, S. D. 57350

SCANDINAVIAN VENISON

venison steaks
1 med. onion, diced
3 tbsp. butter (divided)
½ c. mushrooms, cut up
seasoned flour
1 c. burgundy wine or cooking wine

Cook onion in 1 tbsp. butter over low heat in heavy skillet. Add mushrooms during last minute. Roll venison steaks in well-seasoned flour and brown in hot skillet with at least 2 tbsp. butter.
Combine meat with onion and mushrooms. (Add more seasoning here if you like.) Add burgundy wine or cooking wine, then cover and let simmer until you can pierce the thickest part of the meat with a fork. This will take more than an hour.
Serve with hot bread and tossed green salad.

Mrs. Kermit Karst, 514 Belmont Drive, Rapid City, S. D. 57701

BARBECUED VENISON RIBS

venison ribs
1 med. onion, chopped fine
½ c. vinegar
¼ c. Worcestershire sauce
2 c. boiling water or meat stock
1 c. catsup
2 tbsp. brown sugar
4 tbsp. lemon juice
⅛ tsp. cayenne pepper
2 tbsp. butter or margarine
1 tsp. dry mustard
½ c. celery
1 can tomato sauce
dash of chili powder
1 tbsp. molasses

Heat and pour over raw venison ribs; bake slowly at about 275° for 3-5 hrs., or until well done.
This is a good way to use wild game ribs, which many hunters do not save. Antelope ribs work equally well with this recipe.

Florence Blackburn, Bison, S. D. 57620

BUTTERFLY STEAKS

Cut raw backstrap into 2" slices; slice each piece in half sideways, cutting almost through. Open flat to butterfly. Broil 3 to 4" from heat about 5 min. per side. Brush often with your favorite barbecue sauce.

Mrs. Al Ackerman, North Oxford Road, Aberdeen, S. D. 57401
Mrs. Wayne Hook, RR #3, Huron, S. D. 57350

VENISON SWISS STEAK

2 lbs. venison round steak
flour
salt
pepper
shortening
2 large onions
2 stalks celery, diced
1 c. tomatoes
1 tbsp. Worcestershire sauce
salt and pepper

Dredge steak with flour and season with salt and pepper. Brown in fat; add the rest of the ingredients; cover tightly and cook in a 350° oven for 1¼ hrs. Makes gravy from juice in pan.
Serves 4.

Mrs. Rudy Scholl, RR #1, Box 64, Madison, S. D. 57042

VENISON TERIYAKI

2 lbs. sirloin or round venison, 1½ inches thick
1 can condensed beef consomme
⅓ c. soy sauce
¼ c. chopped onions
1 glove garlic
2 tbsp. lemon juice (can use bottled)
2 tbsp. brown sugar
1 tsp. seasoned salt

Slice meat diagonally across grain ¼ inch thick. Put in large bowl. Mix other ingredients for marinade; pour over meat; refrigerate overnight.
Drain meat; broil 3 to 4 inches from heat about 5 minutes on first side. Baste with marinade. Broil other side 3 minutes, basting. Do not overcook. Heat remaining marinade to pass with meat.
Serves 6.

Mrs. Al Ackerman, North Oxford Road, Aberdeen, S. D. 57401

VENISON DELUXE

¼ c. fat
2 lbs. venison, cubed
1 clove garlic
1 c. diced celery
½ c. onions, chopped
1 c. diced carrots
1 bay leaf
1 tsp. salt
⅛ tsp. pepper
2 c. water
4 tbsp. butter
4 tbsp. flour
1 c. sour cream

Melt fat, add meat and garlic. Brown; arrange in baking dish. Place vegetables in remaining fat—cook 2 min. Add salt, pepper, and water. Pour mixture over meat. Bake at 325° until done. Melt butter in fry pan; stir in flour; add liquid from cooked meat. Boil till thick. Add sour cream. Pour over meat and vegetable mixture.

Mrs. Goerge Vance, Gettysburg, S. D. 57442
Mrs. Oliver Carlson, Seneca, S. D. 57780

VENISON STEAK CASSEROLE

2 lbs. round steak (¾" to 1" thick)
6 tbsp. flour (divided)
1 tsp. salt (divided)
½ tsp. pepper (divided)
⅛ tsp. oregano
1 clove garlic, crushed
3 tbsp. shortening
6 med. potatoes, sliced
2 med. onions, sliced
2 carrots, sliced
1 green pepper, cut in squares
3 c. beef bouillon

Cut steak into serving pieces. Pound in mixture of ¼ c. flour, ½ tsp. salt, pepper, oregano and garlic.
Brown in shortening; place in one layer on bottom of 3 qt. baking dish.
Layer half of potatoes, onion, carrots and pepper on top; sprinkle with half of remaining flour, salt and pepper.
Repeat. Pour bouillon over top. Cover and bake ½ hr. or until vegetables are done (350° oven).

Mrs. Wayne Hook, RR #3, Huron, S. D. 57350
Mrs. Al Ackerman, North Oxford Road, Aberdeen, S. D. 57401

HUNTER'S LODGE ONE DISH MEAL

1½ lb. venison or antelope cubed about ¾"
1 med. to large onion, chopped fine
1 c. celery, diced
butter for browning
½ c. uncooked rice
1 can cream of chicken soup
1 can cream of mushroom soup
1 can mushroom stems and pieces
4 tsp. soy sauce
salt and pepper to taste
1 c. peas
1 c. water

Brown venison, onion and celery in butter. Mix together and add rice, canned soups, mushrooms, soy sauce, and seasonings. Place in casserole. Add 1 c. peas and 1 c. water. Bake in a moderate oven until rice and meat are tender.

Mrs. Russel Jacobs, Box 67, Roslyn, S. D. 57261

VENISON STROGANOFF

1 lb. venison round steak or rump roast
2 cans onion soup
1 12 oz. carton sour cream
1 can mushrooms
butter

Cut meat in thin strips, wrap in foil and bake 1 hour. Add to soup and sour cream and bake 30 minutes. Saute mushrooms in butter before adding to mixture. Serve on wild rice. Half brown rice may be used in place of the wild rice.

**Mrs. Harland Drumm, 1034 Third Street N. E.,
Watertown, S. D. 57201**

ROAST ELK OR VENISON SUPREME

3 to 4 lb. roast
½ c. red cooking wine (divided)
1 tsp. meat tenderizer
2 tsp. salt
2 tsp. pepper
1 tsp. garlic powder
6 thin round slices fresh lemon
4 to 6 slices salt pork

Basting Sauce:
¼ c. butter
¼ c. honey
½ c. frozen orange juice
½ tsp. rosemary

Soak roast in water with ½ c. vinegar over night. Wash and dry well. Brush with wine. Shake on tenderizer, salt, pepper and garlic powder. Place lemon slices on top of roast. Place salt pork on top of lemon slices. Secure with toothpicks. Place in 275° oven 4-5 hrs. In double boiler, melt butter, add honey, orange juice and remainder of wine and rosemary. Baste roast often with this mixture while baking.

Mrs. Dorothy Williams, 10032 Deadwood Ave., Ellsworth AFB, S. D. 57706

Side Dishes

SAVORY RICE BAKE

1 c. dry rice
3 c. water
2 tbsp. dried onion
1 tsp. dried parsley
½ tsp. sage
½ tsp. Spanish rice seasoning
salt
3 to 4 tbsp. butter

Pre-heat oven to 350°. Combine all ingredients in a greased casserole. Bake about 30 min. or until rice feels tender between fingers and all water is absorbed. Stir once or twice during baking.

Variation:
Omit sage, Spanish rice seasoning and salt and substitute ½ tsp. savory salt and ½ tsp. celery salt.

Mrs. L. G. Vanderbush, Clear Lake, S. D. 57226

CURRIED RICE

Accompaniment for venison and antelope roasts, roasted ducks and roasted wild geese.

3 tbsp. fat
1 c. minced onion
1 c. chopped green pepper
½ c. currants
2 c. dry rice
1 tsp. salt
½ tsp. pepper
½ tsp. turmeric
½ tsp. curry powder
1 qt. chicken broth

Saute onion, green pepper and currants. Stir in rice and seasonings; brown slightly. Add chicken broth. Bake in covered casserole in a moderate oven for 30 min.
Serves 8.

Mrs. L. G. Vanderbush, Clear Lake, S. D. 57226

GOLDEN SAFFRON RICE

1½ c. dry rice
6 tbsp. butter
1 tsp. salt
⅛ tsp. saffron, crushed
3 c. canned chicken broth or strained chicken stock or 2 chicken bouillon cubes and water

Cook rice in butter, stirring with fork till golden. Add salt, saffron and broth. Cook over low heat in heavy pan 12-14 minutes or until rice has absorbed broth. For casserole, bake covered in a moderate oven for 45 min.

Mrs. L. G. Vanderbush, Clear Lake, S. D. 57226

HUSH PUPPIES—ACCOMPANIMENT FOR FRIED FISH

2¼ c. self-rising corn meal
3 tbsp. self-rising flour
2-4 tsp. finely chopped onion
1 egg, beaten
1 c. milk

Combine corn meal, flour and chopped onion. Add egg and gradually stir in milk. Drop batter by tablespoonfuls into hot fat. (About 375°) Use the deep fat where fish was fried. Cook until golden brown. Test one to see if it is done in the center. Drain on absorbent paper. Serve at once with fried fish. Makes about 16 small hush puppies.

Mrs. Dave Robin, PO Box 463, Upton, Wyoming 82730

CREAM SAUCE FOR GAME

2 tsp. minced onions
2 tbsp. butter or margarine
2 tsp. flour
1 tsp. lemon juice
1½ c. heavy cream
2 tsp. currant jelly
salt (dash)

After roasting game—remove from pan, pour off fat. Stir in onion, butter, flour; cook about 2 min. Slowly add the cream, then the lemon juice. Cook, stirring until blended and thickened. Add jelly and salt to taste.

Mrs. Silvis Bolden, 1520 South Second Street, Aberdeen, S. D. 57401

FRENCH DIP

If you have wondered what to do with leftover roast from wild game, here is a mighty tasty way to dispose of it. This is also great for beef roasts.

Left-over roast
1 beef bouillon cube
1 can of beef broth (canned store variety)
2 c. water
⅓ c. dry red wine (burgundy, chronti, etc.)
2 tsp. vegetable flakes

Bring the 2 c. water to a boil and dissolve the bouillon cube in it. Add the can of beef broth, the dry wine and the vegetable flakes. (The vegetable flakes can be put in a blender with some of the liquid and be pulverized if you wish). Let this mixture simmer on low heat for ½ hour. Cut the leftover roast in slices as thin as you can make them. After the broth has simmered for ½ hour add the sliced roast and simmer for ten minutes. Now take some poor boy buns; spilt them and butter the inside. Toast them on a hot griddle or under the broiler. To serve take the roast from the broth. Make hot roast beef sandwiches. Serve the broth in cups for each individual and dip the sandwiches in the broth. Each individual should have at least ½ cup of broth.

Mrs. Fred M. Rosin Jr., Pierre, S. D. 57501

SANDWICH FILLING

Can use pheasant, wild goose or other game.
Place in kettle, with a few cups of water, and cook until tender. Remove meat from bone. Grind, and season with salt, pepper and (onion, if desired). Add 1 can of cream of chicken soup undiluted to ground meat to moisten it. Also you may add a little salad dressing if you desire.

Rose Paulsen, RR #1, Miller, S. D. 57362